$Lyme
HOW MEDICAL CODES MORTALLY WOUND CORRUPTION AND SCIENTIFIC FRAUD

Jenna Luché-Thayer

DEDICATION

To my husband Steve, who lived with undiagnosed Lyme for decades and then, at the age of 47, married a woman who thinks a marriage vow means going global in a fight for the human rights of Lyme patients and dinner is bags of salad and nuts thrown across the room.

To my family and friends who failed me, freed me and then joined me.

To all those who defend the human rights for the medically marginalized and fight to overturn healthcare corruption.

Failure is impossible.

CONTENTS

$Lyme
HOW MEDICAL CODES MORTALLY WOUND CORRUPTION AND SCIENTIFIC FRAUD

PART FIVE: ICD11 Whup Ass

Chapter 12: Easy to diagnose, treat & cure

PART SIX: Global Mobilization

ACKNOWLEDGMENTS

I want to thank Ken Liegner for his unshakeable commitment to serving the vulnerable Lyme patient community; he inspired me to take action as an advocate.

Thank you to Joe Burrascano, who freely disseminated his treatment guidelines for Lyme. This guide was used by my nurse practitioner in rural Tennessee to successfully put my late stage and disabling Lyme infection into remission.

Thank you to David Skidmore, an amazingly resilient man who reminded me humor has the power to unmask and vanquish evil. And then reached out to me with the offer to collaborate.

My gratitude to the dynamic mother-daughter team Cozette and Nicole Moysa, my editors at large, allies and friends.

A huge thank you to the extraordinary all-voluntary inter-national Dream Team who contributed to the historic changes in the International Diagnostic Codes for Lyme. Their research helped to shape $Lyme. For additional information on these topics, please read their Reports, entered into UN record in 2017 and 2018.

Updating ICD11 Borreliosis Diagnostic Codes: Edition One, March 29, 2017. ISBN-10: 1978091796, ISBN-13: 978-1978091795. Copyright © 2017 —available on Amazon

The Situation of Human Rights Defenders of Lyme and Relapsing Fever Borreliosis Patients: Edition One, March 6, 2018 ISBN-10: 1722988061, ISBN-13: 978-1722988067. Copyright © 2018 —available on Amazon

Lastly, I want to thank all those who try to interfere with my advocacy work, you are as gasoline is to fire.

Speak the truth but leave immediately after.
Proverb

Or stay
—Jenna Luché-Thayer

PART ONE
The Aha Moment

In a time of deceit telling the truth is a revolutionary act.
—George Orwell

Chapter 1:   Philadelphia 2016

It was a blustery and grey November day in Philadelphia when I met Dr. Ken Liegner at the 2016 annual International Lyme and Associated Diseases Society (ILADS) Conference.

I was pretty thrilled to meet Ken. I had read his book, <u>In the Crucible of Chronic Lyme Disease</u>. Ken's book meticulously details decades of fraudulent science and unethical medical practices. He describes human rights violations inflicted upon persons suffering from Lyme borreliosis—including the medical execution of a woman with validated Lyme infection.

Ken is globally known for advocating against the cruel and inhumane treatment of persons living with the devastations from Lyme and co-infections. He has devoted over 40 years to the medical care of those suffering from illnesses.

I had learned a great deal from Ken's work and the advocacy efforts of others devoted to telling the truth about this illness. I learned that Lyme borreliosis, also known as Lyme disease or Lyme, is caused by *Borrelia* bacteria found throughout the world. Undetected and undertreated Lyme may result in life threatening complications, many neurodegenerative conditions including dementia, and is proven to pass from mother to child with potentially fatal complications.

There are over 300 species of *Borrelia* currently identified in the world, and 103 species are identified as being able to cause infection in humans and warm-blooded animals. New *Borrelia* species and strains continue to be identified and surveillance shows the incidence of borreliosis has increased and spread globally over the past four decades.

Ken is also a long time member of ILADS, one of the only medical societies in the world specializing in treating persons suffering from tickborne diseases.

I was attending the ILADS Conference to gain more medical and scientific knowledge of this complex illness. In 2012, following years of misdiagnoses including lupus and MS, I was finally diagnosed with Lyme.[1]

After six months of antibiotic therapy and other medical treatments, I no longer showed any symptoms of lupus and my three previously diagnosed autoimmune diseases.[2] [3]

My remission gave me a fortunate reprieve from debilitating illness and inspired an obligation to help those obstructed from diagnosis and treatment for borreliosis. This led me to don my 'professional hat' and draw upon my three decades of professional research experience across 42 nations to investigate this situation.

I am a former Senior Advisor to the US government and the United Nations (UN). My expertise includes transparency and accountability, corruption and human rights.[4] I wanted to know why it took me years of effort to obtain the correct diagnosis for this potentially fatal illness. I also wanted to better understand why it was so difficult to access adequate medical care for an illness one can easily contract almost anywhere in the US and in all regions of the world.

Vectors which carry illness, such as mosquitos and ticks, are everywhere and for this reason, vector borne diseases pose a notoriously difficult public health challenge. As an example, nearly half the world's population is at risk of malaria from mosquito bites, and even the best prevention practices only reduce the number of bites. In endemic areas, most people carry malaria, even when they do not have obvious signs of illness.

According to the UN's Children's Fund or UNICEF, over one million people die from malaria each year. Malaria kills one child every 30 seconds and most children are under five years of age. More than 40 percent of the world's population lives in malarial zones and an estimated 300-600 million people are known to experience active infection each year.

I have lived and worked in many malaria endemic areas of the world and at one point in time, diagnostic tests showed I carried four different strains. Even though I carry the malaria infection, I have only had a couple of active cases of the disease. My malaria treatments did not eradicate the pathogens from my body but subdued the infection to the point where I showed no active signs of illness. For this reason, I am not allowed to give blood.

Like mosquitoes, ticks are globally dispersed. Few people know how many mosquito bites they have endured, and few know how many tick bites they have had. Nymphs are immature ticks and they carry many diseases. Nymphs are the size of a poppy seed and may feed on a person, transmit infection and drop off within minutes.

As a child I spent many years in Asia and Africa where there was little medical infrastructure and my parents put heavy emphasis on disease prevention. I have led an active outdoor lifestyle which includes living and working all over the globe in farming communities, hiking through the wilderness, puttering around in my flower garden, camping, sports and picnicking on grassy fields. My many companion pets accompanied me in my outdoor activities. Despite my prevention practices, I have had countless numbers of mosquito bites, tick bites and tick attachments.

My academic major in science, with an emphasis in biology, came in handy for the review of the scientific and medical information regarding Lyme. I understood that, like malaria, my body may continue to carry the infection following treatment. Also like my malaria infections, my Lyme infection can resurface should I not take very good care of myself, suffer significant stress, injury or become infected with other diseases.

I discovered Lyme undermines my immune system, can evade my immune system and antibiotic treatments, and forms biofilms. Antibiotics can kill the outer regions of bacterial biofilms but often cannot penetrate the biofilm to kill the entire infection. There are many pathogens which form biofilms and cause recurring disease because the infection may never become fully eradicated. As an example, biofilms have been found in the ear structures of children with ear infections which recur following multiple treatments.

There are also many infections which are 'treated successfully' but never go away. Such infections become latent, with no clear symptoms, while they quietly continue to do serious damage which will surface later. This is been well documented with tuberculosis, syphilis and with the *Borrelia* bacteria which causes Lyme and Lyme-like illnesses.

There was a good chance I would be reinfected with Lyme even with prevention practices because ticks are everywhere. I had accumulated different strains of malaria by living and working in malarial zones and there was a good chance I would accumulate different strains of *Borrelia* in the future.

As I understood, the only way I could prevent further Lyme infections was to never go outside or allow the outside to come into my home. As someone who loves nature and works across the globe in many rural settings, this was neither desirable nor possible.

In all honesty, I have made no commitment to wearing long pants tucked into socks *every time I go outside*, as is recommended by the Centers for Disease Prevention and Control (CDC) for tick bite prevention. I do, however, use effective tick repellents when I am working outside, and wear long pants tucked into socks when I go hiking and I do tick checks when I come in from the outdoors for both myself and my animals.

I do not have medical confirmation of my first Lyme infection. However, I had 'classic Lyme symptoms' at the age of 16 which were never diagnosed as any particular medical condition. At the time, I was a healthy athletic girl who trained for hours every day as a classical ballerina. I also enjoyed sports and hiking and took care of livestock.

That summer, I caught a flu. A few weeks later, I developed a slight Bell's palsy. For the next three months, I suffered from severe fatigue and overall body pain with significant swelling of my knee and ankle joints. My physician proposed my swollen joints, fatigue and pain were due to my enthusiasm for sports and hiking and recommended I take a break from those activities. Fortunately, after three months, my pain, fatigue and joint swelling subsided, and my Bell's palsy became less perceptible.

This story is not uncommon for those who are diagnosed with late stage systemic Lyme. Although my young immune system was robust, the Lyme infection was already infiltrating every aspect of my physical being and lying in wait for stress or injury, another illness, or the inevitable weakening of my immune system from aging.

Historically, the public health strategies recommended to prevent vector borne diseases include messages for prevention, reliable diagnostics and an array of treatment options. During my research I quickly discovered this was not the case for Lyme and the Lyme-like illnesses caused by borreliosis pathogens.

Studies show that there is a close correlation between the perceived corruption and the actual corruption.
—Transparency International

Chapter 2: Welcome to the World of $Lyme

The 2016 ILADS Conference in Philadelphia was a whirlwind of activity and cutting-edge scientific and medical exchange. Nevertheless, Ken and I continued our conversations regarding the human rights violations against Lyme patients.

I told Ken about my prior successes with regard to establishing the recognition of human rights violations for tough topics such as human trafficking and domestic violence. I asked Ken if we could brainstorm how to address human rights situation surrounding the Lyme epidemic. We both agreed these human rights violations are largely driven by a combination of medical, scientific and insurance fraud.

Winner of American Medical Writers Association Book Award, Pamela Weintraub identifies and describes reasons for this atypical public health response in her book, <u>Lyme Cure Unknown: Inside the Lyme Epidemic</u>. This book reveals how the role of insurance fraud and profiteering denies medical care for this patient group and describes other indications of corruption.

My research found the scope of fraud and corruption is global and many government institutions and government officials are complicit in its practice. This includes a wide range of corrupted disease surveillance and diagnostic practices to support the denial of the epidemic.

There are billions in profits being made by treating borreliosis patients with non-curative and dangerous symptom-modifying drugs. Simultaneously, the medical costs of validated treatment options are offloaded onto those suffering from persistent, late stage and complicated forms of the disease.

Collusion runs rampant to maintain this denial and these profit schemes.

Welcome to the world of $Lyme.

*If one is lucky, a solitary fantasy can totally
transform one million realities.*
—Maya Angelou

Chapter 3: The Aha Moment

Ken and I continued our conversation following the Philadelphia ILADS Conference. I called him from sunny Florida that winter and he called me from cold, snowy upstate New York. Between our phone conversations, I continued to research the global fraud, corruption and human rights violations surrounding the Lyme epidemic.

One afternoon in early December 2016, Ken shared his frustration regarding the extremely limited code choices in the medical software for making a differential diagnosis for Lyme.

The patient's symptoms are entered into the medical software system. The software matches the group of symptoms entered by the doctor and provides a list of possible medical diagnoses with corresponding medical codes. These medical software systems are used throughout the United States and much of the world. The codes assigned to specific diagnoses are also used by insurance systems and government-sponsored healthcare in many countries for the allocation of treatment and reimbursement of medical costs.

The available symptom list compatible with a Lyme diagnosis presents symptoms occurring in the acute phase of infection, while many symptoms common to later stages are absent from the software system. This means even though there is a code of Lyme polyneuropathy, the code was underutilized because polyneuropathy is not described as an acute symptom of the illness.

The software system is not set up to arrive at a diagnosis of many of the serious and life threatening complications caused by Lyme. The lack of representation of these numerous complications from Lyme means these late stage and chronic forms of the illness cannot not be entered into the medical software system.

Additionally, the diagnostic codes for many Lyme complications are nonexistent; therefore, the treatments for these serious complications are also missing from the software used by most practitioners. The situation was a classic Catch-22.

Ken then referred to the medical codes as 'ICD codes'...

... and that was the aha moment.

As a former Senior Advisor to the UN, I am very familiar with the World Health Organization (WHO). Additionally, my UN posts had made me extremely knowledgeable about the UN requirements for stakeholder processes. WHO is part of the UN system and implements a comprehensive global stakeholder process for International Classification of Diseases codes, otherwise known as ICD codes.

ICD codes are used globally to identify and record diseases, injuries and deaths. In many countries, ICD codes are tied to insurance plans and reimbursement for medical care.

I realized we had the potential to effect global benefits for Lyme patients if we could successfully engage the right mix of stakeholders in the ICD revisions.

Success would mean millions of persons suffering from late stage and persistent disease complications could potentially gain access to diagnosis and treatment options which meet internationally accepted standards!

Barring interference from corruption, new Lyme codes for late stage and persistent disease complications could overturn decades of medical marginalization and the human rights abuse of this patient group.

New Lyme codes would obligate insurance companies and national health systems to recognize and cover the treatments for late stage, complicated and persistent forms of this infection!

Chance favors the prepared mind.
—Louis Pasteur

Chapter 4: The Dream Team

How exciting to realize changing the ICD codes for Lyme could potentially increase access to Lyme diagnosis and treatment on a global scale!

Creating these ICD code changes, however, was going to be a tremendous undertaking. Historically, ICD codes have been revised approximately once every ten years. Fortunately, WHO was still in the end phase of the eleventh revision of the ICD or ICD11. According to the WHO calendar, all recommendations for the ICD11 revision were due by March 30, 2017.

Would it be possible to make radical changes to the ICD codes for Lyme by the March 30, 2017 deadline?

Yes! But this could only happen if highly skilled and dedicated individuals would be willing to volunteer their time. Not only did we need a Dream Team, we needed a Dream Team which could successfully navigate the treacherous pitfalls created by corruption.

International representation is critically necessary when working on global issues such as the borreliosis pandemic. Multiregional representation in a stakeholder group is required for credibility with WHO and other UN entities.

I asked Ken and a few trusted advocates if they would like to form an informal all-voluntary committee to change the ICD11 codes for Lyme. I also asked allies to recommend and help recruit medical and scientific professionals to join our Dream Team and urged they reach out to every corner of the globe.

Before the end of January 2017, our informal and all-voluntary Dream Team membership included highly skilled professionals from North America, the Asia Pacific region, Africa, South America and Eastern, Western and Northern Europe.

Many members are scientific and medical experts who have worked on borreliosis for two and three decades. The Dream Team members have conducted many studies and published many hundreds of peer-reviewed publications. They serve as leaders, clinicians and professors across numerous well respected academic and research centers.

We have members who consult regularly to WHO and governments on the development of health systems, surveillance practices, patient-centered care, ageing, zoonosis and other specialized areas. Other members are experts in law, governance, accountability, institutional reform, climate change, capacity building and human rights. We also have members who have worked extensively with the private sector, from multinational corporations in multiple countries to local private education centers.

Our Dream Team was assembled and ready to roll.

One might think this group could easily improve the ICD codes for Lyme. However, in January 2017, the ICD codes for Lyme had hardly changed in the decades they had been part of the code system. The reasons for this stagnation had nothing to do with science and medicine —and everything to do with fraud and corruption.

$Lyme is the fraud and corruption surrounding the global Lyme and borreliosis epidemic. Our $Lyme opponents are powerful, numerous and heavily supported by the some of the most powerful institutions on the planet. They include the insurance and pharmaceutical industries, with tentacles spanning across numerous medical societies, academic and government institutions.

$Lyme also includes governments unwilling to cover the medical costs of their infected military, their infected employees and their infected citizens.

$Lyme is very Ugly and very Global.

By repetition,
each lie becomes an irreversible fact
upon which other lies are constructed.
—John Le Carré

PART TWO
The World of $Lyme

*Corruption is a problem because
it dilutes confidence in democracy's main institutions
and violates fundamental equality principles.*
— Transparency International

Chapter 5: Global Corruption in the Health Sector

On October 24, 2017, the UN Special Rapporteur on the right to health, Dainius Pūras, presented a special report on corrupttion to the UN General Assembly. The Special Rapporteur told his audience,

"In many countries, health is among the most corrupt sectors; this has significant implications for equality and non-discrimination"

The Special Rapporteur emphasized the 'normalization' of institutional corruption in the healthcare sector and the corrupting force of the global pharmaceutical industry. He then detailed many illegal acts and practices currently undermining medical ethics, effective healthcare provision, social justice and transparency.

Many researchers support the Special Rapporteur's findings. Dr. Peter C. Gøtzsche, the former Director of the Nordic Cochrane Centre in Copenhagen, Denmark has done significant research on the global corruption of medical care by big Pharma.[5] Gøtzsche has published widely read books on the subject such as <u>Deadly Medicines and Organized Crime</u>. He and other scholars have lectured on the corporatization of medical practice and how this has contributed to the undermining of ethical practices and the loss of medical professional autonomy.

Martin Shkreli, OxyContin and EpiPens are names which resonate with healthcare corruption. Martin Shkreli, the former CEO of Turing Pharmaceuticals, was globally criticized when Turing obtained the manufacturing license for the antiparasitic drug Daraprim and raised the price from $13.50 to $750 per tablet. Daraprim treats conditions affecting HIV patients and other persons with weakened immune systems.

EpiPens contain life-saving medication for those with potentially fatal allergies. Marketed by Mylan, there is little competition. A two-pack of the epinephrine-filled devices cost $56.64 wholesale in 2007 and by 2016, Mylan increased its price to $365.16— an increase of almost 550 percent.

Purdue Pharma has earned roughly $35 billion in opioid manufacturing and sales of OxyContin. The company falsely marketed the opioid as low risk for addiction. Sales grew from $48 million in 1996 to almost $1.1 billion in 2000. By 2004, OxyContin had become a leading drug of abuse in the United States.

In an April 10, 2018 Report to health sector clients, Goldman Sachs analyst Salveen Richter asked '*Is curing patients a sustainable business model?*' Salveen then answered '*cures for diseases are not great for business —more specifically, they are bad for long term profits*'. The Report suggested profits would be better served by focusing on prevalent diseases or conditions, such as treatments for the 'disease of aging'.

Besides Salveen and Goldman Sachs, who knew aging was a disease?

In September 2018, the top physician at Memorial Sloan Kettering Cancer Center in New York was found to have failed to disclose millions in financial ties to industry and ownership interests in health care companies. Dr. José Baselga received millions of dollars in consulting fees and routinely failed to disclose these relationships at scientific conferences and in journal articles. As of September 18, 2018, the hospital's CEO has taken no clear corrective measures against these corrupting practices.

The $Lyme found in the Lyme and borreliosis epidemic is not quite so conspicuous, flashy or simple as these cases of corruption. Furthermore, $Lyme corruption results in little to no media coverage.

As an example, on November 10, 2017, a group of Lyme patients filed a federal antitrust and racketeering lawsuit in the U.S. District Court for the Eastern District of Texas, Texarkana Division —Case 5:17-cv-00190-RWS against the Infectious Diseases Society of America (IDSA). The patients alleged major health insurers are denying coverage for Lyme treatments based on factitious Guidelines established by their paid IDSA consultants.

The antitrust case detailed how more than 50 physicians in New York, New Jersey, Connecticut, Michigan, Oregon, Rhode Island and Texas were investigated, disciplined or had their licenses removed for speaking out against these Guidelines. According to the lawsuit, from 1997 to 2000, many of these doctors were reported to their medical boards by insurance companies.

This antitrust lawsuit contains many components which would normally attract national media attention. The story involves powerful industries pitted against the average person, an uncontrolled epidemic sweeping across the nation, and a cliff hanger—everyone is at risk for this infection and may be denied treatment.

Why was this story ignored by the same media covering other healthcare corruption stories?

One reason may be the insurance industry *is the most powerful industry globally* and buys influence to discourage media coverage of its widespread fraud and corruption.

Both health insurers and disability insurers actively avoid compensating Lyme patients. Back in 2016, Jane Furer, an NBC platform manager for Comcast, contacted me to investigate her denial of long-term disability benefits from MetLife. I found MetLife had used one of the doctors commonly contracted by insurers to deny Lyme diagnosis, late stage complications from Lyme and persistent Lyme and, therefore, deny any related disability benefits.

The denial of Jane's benefits resulted in a financial situation which forced Jane to return to work against her treating physician's recommendations. Jane's health subsequently deteriorated after her premature return to work. She was diagnosed with autoimmune encephalitis, seizure disorder and atrial ventricular (AV) heart block. Apparently, MetLife may have lied about not receiving documents for her current claim.

$Lyme Actors include the pharmaceutical industry, insurance and disability companies and their shills. Had I accepted my diagnosis of multiple sclerosis (MS) and lupus, I would have been put on very expensive 'symptom modifying drugs' for the rest of my miserable life. These drugs, also known as biologics, are not curative and are routinely prescribed for the growing number of chronic degenerative diseases of 'unknown cause'.

Many biologics are immunosuppressive. If I had taken MS and lupus drugs, my systemic Lyme infection would have destroyed my health even further.

Biologics are proving to be the golden goose of the pharmaceutical industry. Pharma would have earned roughly $50,000 per year for treatment of my chronic symptoms. By 2018, Pharma would have sold me well over half a million dollars in drugs which would have further damaged my body.

Sorry Pharma! I found out I had late stage Lyme. The infection was successfully treated with generic antibiotics, costing roughly $1000 over a six month period. Pharma lost 'a patient profit center' which could have lined their pockets with more than a million dollars.

Lyme and Lyme-like illnesses caused by other borreliosis pathogens are found throughout the globe. Just imagine the millions of undiagnosed and wrongly diagnosed persons benefiting Pharma, while their health is being harmed by expensive, ineffective and dangerous drugs.

Of course, I know I am extremely fortunate. Many persons suffering from late stage, complicated and persistent forms of the disease are not diagnosed. Many of those able to secure a diagnosis cannot access treatment options which meet internationally validated standards. Among those able to access these treatment options, many require ongoing therapies to manage their symptoms.

Beyond Pharma, $Lyme has a multilayered cast of characters. $Lyme has many Actors, individuals and institutions, both private and public, who are making unknown billions via conflicts of interest and collusion. The lack of ICD codes have reflected and supported this scientific and medical fraud and corruption. Some of the $Lyme Actors are indeed methodical; however, they are joined by opportunistic predators, including those you might never consider.

*The controversy in Lyme disease research is
a shameful affair. And I say that because the whole thing
is politically tainted. Money goes to people who have, for the
past 30 years, produce the same thing —nothing.*
—Willy Burgdorfer,
discoverer of Lyme bacteria

Chapter 6: The Infectious Diseases Society of America (IDSA) & Their Global $Lyme Allies

The IDSA is a private medical society which exerts powerful influence over both US domestic and global health policies. The IDSA has a significant advisory role for the US Department of Defense (DOD). Many government officials responsible for Lyme and tickborne diseases are members of the IDSA. This private medical society has enmeshed affiliations with two of the most powerful sectors, insurance and pharmaceutical. The IDSA has a long-established history of promoting legislation and policies which financially benefits its membership.[6]

I personally know IDSA members with great integrity, and I am sure there are many upstanding professionals in the IDSA. $Lyme, however, appears to compromise many people. There are infectious disease doctors who treat themselves and family members with antibiotic cocktails and long-term antibiotics to treat Lyme. Yet, these same doctors will not offer the same treatment options to their patients for fear of attacks by insurance companies and certain powerful members of the IDSA.

The 2006 IDSA Lyme Guidelines are controversial and widely contested for many reasons. From the 1990s through 2007, 202 patents related to *Borrelia* were granted to IDSA members and their affiliates in government and private organizations. These patent holders include authors and contributors to the 2006 IDSA Lyme Guidelines and US government officials.

Most of these conflicts of interests were not disclosed in the development of the 2006 IDSA Lyme Guidelines.[7] (See following table.) This situation was elaborated as a case study in conflicts of interest, medical and scientific bias and other poor practices in the Institute of Medicine's (IOM) 2011 <u>Clinical Practice Guidelines We Can Trust</u>.[8]

Many of these Lyme patents describe an infection, which is barely recognizable, as compared to the disease described in the 2006 IDSA Lyme Guidelines. As an example, Guideline co-author Raymond J. Dattwyler filed a Lyme patent one year following the 2006 Guidelines. The patent states,

"Currently, Lyme Disease is treated with a range of antibiotics ... However, such treatment is not always successful in clearing the infection. Treatment is often delayed due to improper diagnosis with the deleterious effect that the infection proceeds to a chronic condition, where treatment with antibiotics is often not useful ... One of the factors contributing to delayed treatment is the lack of effective diagnostic tools".
[9]

IDSA Members & Affiliates Holding Lyme Related Patents in 2007	
*Raymond J. Dattwyler (US & foreign) *Stephen Dumler (US patents) Alan Barbour (US & foreign) Stanley Stein & Hoffman-Laroche Ira Schwartz & New York Medical College Avant Immunotherapeutics Aventis Pasteur Baxter Becton-Dickinson Boston Medical Center Corp. Biomerieux Cambridge Biotech Centers for Disease Prevention & Control Columbia University Immunetics Johns Hopkins University Mayo Clinic Medimmune & Aventis, University of Minnesota Medimmune	National Institutes of Health & National Institute of Allergies & Infectious Diseases New York Medical College Pasteur Merieux/Connaught Rx Technologies SmithKline Beecham (under GlaxoSmith Kline) State of Rhode Island Stony Brook University (SUNY) Texas A&M University Tufts New England Medical Center Tufts US patents with Partech & GlaxoSmithKline Tulane University University of California University of Connecticut US Army & US Department of Health & Human Services (HHS) Vical Inc. Viro Dynamics Yale University & Yale's Office of Cooperative Research Patents
*co-authors undisclosed COIs during the 2006 IDSA Lyme Guidelines development	

In stark contrast to the disease description found in the majority of the 202 Lyme patents, the IDSA Guidelines claim Lyme is 'easily diagnosed, treated and cured'.[10]

It simply makes no sense that an illness described as 'easily diagnosed, treated and cured' would capture decades of interest by the DOD and other federal agencies, and devour millions of dollars in government research grants.

$Lyme is Big Business —and so are $Lyme patents.

Between 2007 and 2016, approximately 950 US government grants for *Borrelia* were awarded. The institutions affiliated with the authors of the 2006 IDSA Lyme Guideline received approximately two-thirds more grants than other institutions. These grantees have benefited from a steady flow of money and have enjoyed privileged entitlement to publishing on the topic.

Despite this steady stream of money and privilege, the science, recommended testing and treatment presented in the 2006 IDSA Guidelines is almost identical to the original 2000 IDSA Guidelines —and is still being promoted by IDSA in 2018.

No advances in 18 years —except in the numbers of debilitated, disabled and dead persons.

The numbers of IDSA members and their affiliates who have made a career from $Lyme dollars without advancing im-provements in diagnostics and treatments remains unknown.

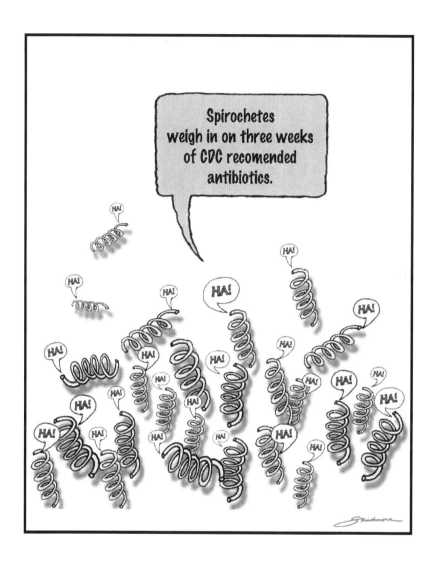

As awareness of the borreliosis pandemic increases, the IDSA has positioned itself to expand a wider reaching influence. According to European medical and scientific professionals, the IDSA favored the creation of a European Union Concerted Action on Lyme Borreliosis (EUCALB).

EUCALB had significant influence over medical societies and national reference centers for Lyme. EUCALB promoted the IDSA Lyme Guidelines and other recommendations.

EUCALB recommended European Union (EU) countries limit their confirmations of Lyme infection to 'at most, five percent' —regardless of the actual numbers or percentage of Lyme infections. The website of EUCALB disappeared in 2017
— shortly after the racketeering lawsuit against the IDSA was filed.

The European Society of Clinical Microbiology and Infectious Diseases' (ESCMID) Study Group for Lyme Borreliosis (ESGBOR) is currently influencing most policies and practices related to Lyme. Gerold Stanek (Austria) is a co-author of the 2006 IDSA Lyme Guidelines and treasurer of the 2018 ESGBOR Executive Committee —Chairperson Ram B. Dessau (Denmark) and Secretary Tobias Rupprecht, (Germany) also echo IDSA Lyme opinions.

Susan O'Connell is the former manager of the Lyme Disease Reference Laboratory at Southampton. Susan claimed that 'Europe supports IDSA Lyme Guidelines in a 2010 presentation to UK officials. Susan was "most grateful" to Guidelines authors John Halperin, Gary Wormser, Gerold Stanek and ESGBOR Executive Committee's Chairperson Ram Dessau in her acknowledgements.

Susan played an active $Lyme role by reporting UK doctors of Lyme patients who tested positive at her laboratory. By 2012, Susan's laboratory was found to have falsified accreditation and many other serious violations. These include the destruction of test documentation and diagnosing cerebrospinal fluid (CSF) with a test only certified for blood.

The UK laboratory was closed in 2012. Susan was reported to have retired with a £40,000 bonus (55,523.60 US dollars) and went to work for Baxter on their Lyme vaccine. Baxter has been in business with some of the Guideline's authors.

These scenarios represent only a small portion of the conflicts of interests and web of relationships and collusion between the IDSA and affiliates across the globe.

[Lyme] Serology has to be started from scratch with people who don't know beforehand the results of their research.
—Willy Burgdorfer

Chapter 7: $Lyme and Diagnostic Testing

Lyme diagnostic testing is one of the most dependable profit streams for many $Lyme Actors and every effort is made to maintain the status quo. There are already superior diagnostic options to the $Lyme recommended tests that detect immune response (serology).

Aggressive efforts to protect existing profit streams include the suppression of diagnostic technologies which are far more accurate. They include attacks on persons and organizations which develop and compete with the standard serology tests.

According to Paul Auwaerter, the current IDSA President,

"[Lyme] serologic test inherently is not able to distinguish active versus past infection ... current [Lyme] serologic tests work best for patients who have symptoms beyond the first two to four weeks as this is the typical response time for the human immune system to make antibodies against a pathogen ... the development, validation and commercial distribution of new tests can take years and millions of dollars." [11]

The President of the IDSA, an organization globally renown for saying this disease is easy to diagnose, treat and cure, is also claiming the serology tests they promote as 'gold standard' are clearly limited.

Paul is on public record for dismissing all other competing Lyme diagnostic tools which meet required state, national, regional or global standards. There are IDSA members and $Lyme affiliates who stand to lose millions in market share if these competing technologies are not actively slandered, libeled and suppressed.

*If we've been bamboozled long enough,
we tend to reject any evidence of the bamboozle.
We're no longer interested in finding out the truth.
The bamboozle has captured us.*
—Carl Sagan

Number 1: Lie and Deny, Deny, Deny

The promotion of unreliable tests is part of $Lyme's multi-decade status quo strategy to deny the range and numbers of the epidemic, while ensuring profits from the misdiagnosis of millions of persons.

Every time CDC and IDSA, and those who follow their lead, claim Lyme is easily diagnosed, they are misleading and endangering the public.

A meta-analysis and other studies have shown CDC and IDSA recommended serology tests for Lyme have an approximate reliability of 50 percent for males and a 40 percent reliability rate for females.[12] [13]

The blood serological tests for Lyme are much less reliable than the tests for tuberculosis and other potentially fatal infectious diseases. An HIV antibody can be detected in more than 99 percent of infected persons. The third generation of hepatitis C serology tests has a sensitivity of approximately 98 percent. The sensitivity of tuberculosis serological tests range from 1 to 60 percent and the specificity from 53 to 99 percent. The tuberculosis serological tests are widely recognized as unreliable.

Where is the accountability for the $Lyme diagnostic science promoted by CDC, National Institutes of Health (NIH) and their private sector partners?

Over the last couple of years, Lyme patients in an increasing number of countries are taking this scientific and marketing fraud to court. Furthermore, they are winning these cases. The following example is from France:

A wheelchair-bound patient long diagnosed with neuro-degenerative disease had received a negative Lyme serology test like those promoted by Yale, IDSA and CDC. She discovered the standard serology tests for Lyme were unreliable. She then masqueraded as a dog and was able to access polymerase chain reaction (PCR) testing from a veterinary lab. (PCR Lyme blood tests for humans are not covered by most national or private insurers.) Her PCR test result was positive for borreliosis.

After three months of Lyme treatment by renowned Lyme physician, Professor Christian Perronne, she left her wheel-chair and began to ski again. She also lodged a legal complaint against the laboratory for 'aggravated deceit'.

Every time representatives from CDC or IDSA claim the serology tests for Lyme diagnosis are *FDA approved*, they are misleading and endangering the public. These serology tests are *FDA cleared*, but not *FDA approved*. This is an important distinction because FDA approved requires a *far more rigorous review process* than FDA cleared. FDA cleared simply means the Lyme serology tests are substantially equivalent to similar and other legally marketed and sold devices.

According to FDA records, between 1998 and 2018, no less than 43 Lyme diagnostic tests have been FDA cleared. This means the public has been peddled the same diagnostic tests over and over and over —for 30 years. Tests which have the reliability of a coin toss are routinely used to deny diagnosis and treatment.

The corruption surrounding these tests began in the early 1990s, when a small group of government officials colluded with the private sector to remove the most reliable biomarkers from Lyme serology tests. The removal of the biomarker from the test was required to allow for the development of a Lyme vaccine.[14] The new tests were less sensitive and therefore fewer cases would be diagnosed and treated. The new tests, with the removed biomarker, could however, be used to test those who had been vaccinated for Lyme.

The case definition for Lyme was also revised and narrowed during this time. The new case definition emphasized symptoms which were notable but not particularly common. The restricted case definition meant many persons with neurological and other complications, would no longer meet the case definition. Fewer Lyme diagnoses meant a larger pool of potential clients for the vaccine.

Imugen, Yale's L2 Diagnostics and Corixa partnered on the new diagnostic test and advertised the tests would be compatible for the vaccinated population. The partners apparently anticipated many millions would be vaccinated, and they would secure an almost complete monopoly on the Lyme diagnostic business. Their expectations were not met when, within a short period of time following the launch of SmithKline Beecham's Lyme vaccine (LYMErix), over 1000 adverse reactions were reported to the FDA. SmithKline Beecham paid nearly one million dollars in settlement fees.

LYMErix was withdrawn from the market, but we are still stuck with these unacceptably lousy tests and a misleading case definition which excludes many infected with the disease.

It is not uncommon for persons who test Lyme positive to say they had anywhere from five to 10 tests before achieving a positive test result. The costs of Lyme serological tests are not cheap. However, because of their low reliability, people often spend many hundreds of dollars out-of-pocket in the hopes of securing a positive result which will open access to medical treatment.

Imagine having to pay many hundreds of dollars out-of-pocket for 5 to 10 tests for any other common and life threatening disease? The matching of unreliable serology tests to a potentially disabling and fatal disease is a fantastic formula to ensure profits.

It appears no less than 43 companies have found this profit formula very appealing. The FDA records only represent companies promoting tests in the US. There are many other companies across the globe reaping huge profits from peddling pricey unreliable tests to sick and vulnerable people willing to pay multiple times for a result which may allow access to generic antibiotics.

Number 2: Attack Technical Advances & Eliminate Market Competition

The Yale Medical Group has focused on serology-based tests to diagnose Lyme at the 'convalescent stage' of the infection. Convalescence is the later stage of an infectious disease when the patient may be recovering but is still infected and may be a source of infection to others.

Rheumatologists specialize in providing supportive therapy for Lyme infection, rather than controlling or eradicating the infection. Lyme patients are a major source of business for the rheumatologists in Lyme endemic areas. For 30 years, both rheumatologists and Pharma have profited from the prescribing of pain killers, immunosuppressants, symptom modifying drugs and/or biologics for ongoing complications.

At the age of 85, Dr. Sin Hang Lee has long experience with $Lyme. Lee was on the faculty of Yale University and Yale's rheumatology department is credited with discovering and naming Lyme disease.

On September 5, 2018, television station Fox5NY presented the 'Lyme and Reason: Battles and Breakthroughs Against Lyme Disease' and featured Sin Hang Lee's heroic efforts to overcome obstacles to Lyme diagnosis.[15]

Lee was determined to use the best science for early detection of Lyme. In 2004, Lee began to use the 'Sanger sequencing PCR technology' to diagnose Lyme and Lyme-like illnesses. At the time Lee began to adapt the Sanger technology for Lyme, he was a pathologist at Milford Hospital in Connecticut. Lyme is widespread and endemic in this area. In 2008, the hospital's pathology staff and emergency room doctors started testing emergency room patients who might have Lyme.

Lee and his colleagues were the first to develop Sanger PCR with DNA sequencing to diagnose the pathogens in the patient's blood, joint fluid and CSF. The Milford Lyme test was State approved for patient care in 2009.

In contrast to Yale's Lyme serology tests, Lee's technology can diagnose the infection before Lyme antibodies become measurable. Early detection and antimicrobial treatment greatly reduce damage from disseminated infection.

In 2010, Milford Hospital gained their new Chairperson from the Yale Medical Group. The Chairperson told the Milford human resources director to fire Lee because 'Yale's serology-based Lyme diagnostic tests could not compete with the nested PCR/DNA sequencing test to diagnose Lyme disease at early stage of infection'.

Lee was then fired from his job.

Despite this groundbreaking technological advancement for the diagnosis of Lyme, Milford Hospital stopped offering the nested PCR/DNA test. Milford Hospital later rescinded their termination order following a legal complaint by Lee.

Lee continued his work on the nested PCR/DNA test as part of a CDC project comparing current serology Lyme tests to nested PCR/DNA tests. According to CDC, the diagnosis of relapsing fever borreliosis "*currently relies on the use of tests to detect DNA of the organism* such as *Borrelia miyamotoi.*"[16] In 2014, CDC abruptly closed this project with no reason given.

Lee filed a $57 million lawsuit against CDC. The suit alleges the "*CDC implemented an anti-competitive campaign to stifle the use and availability of his DNA-based direct test to diagnose Lyme disease*".

Lee plans to use future awards from this lawsuit to assist laboratories and hospitals make use of this superior technology. Meanwhile, any person who was denied access to his tests can make use of his lawsuit's legal documentation to sue CDC for damages. Obstruction to Lee's tests means untold numbers of infected persons are being denied the right to diagnosis and treatment.

Following the FOX5 interview, Lee sent me a message saying CDC could have attempted to use the FOX5 episode to destroy his *"credibility and legal argument"* —they appear unable to have done so.

Note: In many communications and public statements, Lee has emphasized his many good experiences collaborating with some very fine CDC scientists. I also know dedicated CDC scientists from my international work. I have seen them provide care in many places with little medical infrastructure and threatened by widespread outbreaks of serious diseases. I have seen them work tirelessly to stem epidemics and strengthen medical infrastructure in Africa and Asia.

Many federal agencies have been affected by the Bayh Doyle Act. This Act has resulted in the US being the only industrialized wealthy nation which allows its government officials to derive personal financial benefits from patents they secure while in public office. Unfortunately, laws passed under the Bayh Doyle Act are corrupting the medical and scientific work of our public institutions.

In many cases, patent-holding government officials are allowed to pass judgment on competing technologies. This is a shameful conflict of interest. Such practices destroy the integrity of US government agencies responsible for medicine and science. Government officials (some retired) from both CDC and NIH hold personal business stakes in $Lyme serology tests and patents.

In 2017, I had an unofficial exchange with a senior official from the UN's World Intellectual Property Organization (WIPO). WIPO was created in 1967 'to encourage creative activity, to promote the protection of intellectual property throughout the world'.

According to the senior official, *'the US government's patent corruption is undermining medical and scientific integrity across the globe'*.

I'm not a fan of facts. You see, facts can change,
but my opinion will never change,
no matter what the facts are.
—Stephen Colbert

Chapter 8: Fabricate Fraudulent Syndromes to Deny Medical care for Biological Illness

Post Treatment Lyme Disease Syndrome

There are many well documented strategies of the tactics employed by insurance companies and governments to deny medical care. One of these nefarious tricks is Post Treatment Lyme Disease $yndrome or PTLD$.

As an example, the US military long denied the disabling and life threatening effects of Agent Orange, a toxin used in Southeast Asia during the Vietnam war era. Vietnam era veterans were damaged and dying from their exposure to this poison while the US government successfully offloaded billions of dollars in healthcare responsibilities on to the veterans and their families.

There are many well publicized stories of insurance executives ordering their employees to deny coverage multiple times with the expectation most persons, particularly ill persons, will not pursue reimbursements after repeated denials. Such unethical practices improve the profits of insurance companies.

Many hundreds of thousands of persons in the US have become debilitated and disabled by Lyme. They routinely experience obstruction to treatment options which meet international standards and treatment failure from one-size-fits-all protocols. Estimated millions more have been physically devasted by this disease worldwide.[17]

PTLD$ appears to have been invented in response to the burgeoning population with persistent Lyme. The escalating evidence of the failure of IDSA's recommended Lyme treatment and the costs of the growing numbers of chronically ill Lyme patient must be denied by $Lyme .

PTLD$ is not a disease; it is a 'syndrome' based on a repudiated psychosomatic condition referred to as 'medically unexplained syndrome' or MUS.[18]

PTLD$ promotes the fraud that persons suffering from systemic infection and physical damages from rampant infection are not biologically ill. These patients are falsely labeled as somatic or hypochondriacs.

PTLD$ is an intentional redefining of an illness which is immunosuppressive and difficult to eradicate with antibiotics.

The deliberate mislabeling assists CDC and other government health institutions across the globe in their efforts to deny the epidemic, the unreliability of the standard serology tests and treatment failures of the IDSA Lyme Guidelines.

PTLD$ is an entirely baseless medical fiction.

By adopting PTLD$, governments responsible for tax-based universal healthcare systems can swap the high costs of medical treatments for Lyme complications for the relatively minimal costs of palliative care. This switcheroo saves millions or billions of healthcare dollars, depending on the size of the country. Private insurers also make out like bandits and enrich their bottom line by swallowing PTLD$.

Palliative care is used for those suffering somatic illnesses such as hypochondria and for those who have serious and incurable illnesses. Palliative care does not try to treat or cure the underlying disease; it focuses on providing relief from the symptoms, pain, and mental stress caused by the illness. The commonly used tools of palliative care include antidepressants, counseling and pain management.

Ken Liegner's and Pamela Weintraub's books describe how this denial of medical care for Lyme patients by insurance companies was systematically orchestrated. The antitrust case against the IDSA provides compelling documentation of further collusion and corruption.

Both CDC and NIH have endorsed the fraudulent PTLD$ label, as have government health institutions in other countries. Furthermore, the NIH finances many grantees and articles which promote this fraud. In 2016, IDSA Lyme guideline author Gary Wormser, received one and a half million dollars in taxpayer money to undertake research on the 'subjective symptoms' found in PTLD$.

A one and a half million dollar investment by NIH to maintain the PTLD$ myth means *billions in profits* to the insurance and pharmaceutical industries. This also means minimizing the government's medical costs for any employee sickened by this illness. These include the huge numbers of park service and military personnel who risk constant exposure in the course of their required field exercises.

Articles by NIH grantees characterize persons suffering from persistent and complicated cases of Lyme as being simultaneously 'dangerous but pitiful', 'helpless but powerful', incapable of understanding science yet sufficiently cunning to promote scientific propaganda. These grantees and articles also claim Lyme advocates are controlled by anonymous and well-financed shadowy puppeteers.[19]

Other articles, such as the 2009 article Implications of Gender in Chronic Lyme Disease, by Eugene Shapiro and IDSA Guidelines author Gary Wormser, spurt unfounded gender bias against females. They trumpet PTLD$ as a form of hypochondria, delusions and attention-seeking hysteria and which is more commonly diagnosed in women than men.

These government-sponsored maligners of a vulnerable patient population include IDSA Lyme Guidelines authors and the President of the IDSA. To date, more than $33 million in NIH grants have sponsored tripe masquerading as medical articles.[20]

As of September 14, 2018, CDC and NIH continue to hawk and fund the fraud of PTLD$.

There appear to be misguided souls who believe compromise will change the meaning of PTLD$. It appears they 'believe' linking the term to the many immunological, inflammatory and neurological irregularities caused by persistent infection will overturn $Lyme's intentions.

Their compromise may gain them a seat at $Lyme's table or more. However, their attempts to transform PTLD$ into a viable medical term has failed. Their use of the fraudulent term appears to compromise their professional integrity.

CDC and NIH websites continue to promote PTLD$ as a trivial psychosomatic problem and recommend the reader review the opinions of the commercial, profit-making medical guidance service called 'UptoDate'.[21]

Wolters Kluwer N.V. is a global information services company headquartered the Netherlands and owns UpToDate. The company uses an advanced form of data mining and algorithms to share information across clients from the legal, business, tax, accounting, finance, audit, risk, compliance, and healthcare markets. The company operates in over 150 countries.

Wolters Kluwer is actively limiting independent clinical decision-making choices by reducing 'unwarranted' variations in care. According to their own statements, they emphasize cost-containment in medical care over other factors, such as the best care for the individual patient.

This octopus of a company promises to help physicians by undertaking nearly all the decision-making required of a medical professional. The medical professional can now let Wolters Kluwer take over every task for which they trained, from evaluating symptoms and test results, to diagnosing the condition, to deciding next steps regarding treatments. It appears Wolters Kluwer/UpToDate offers 'cookbook medicine' in exchange for clinical judgment.

Why is a private multinational conglomerate —concerned with cost containment and profit making across healthcare markets and other businesses— being promoted by the US government to give medical guidance for any illness, including Lyme?

UpToDate's guidance on Lyme and a multitude of illnesses cause concern. Perhaps they would better be named 'Out of Date' or 'We Peddle Schlock'?

Immoral practices related to denying diagnosis and treatment have high costs. Recent calculations have found Lyme to be costing the US between $25 and $75 billion per year.[22]

$Lyme helps some make billions while costing billions to the nation.

There are three kinds of lies:
lies, damned lies, and statistics.
—Mark Twain

Chapter 9: Falsify the Numbers &
Delete the Category

$Lyme practices are very thorough and include the suppression of epidemiological information regarding Lyme. The case definition for Lyme was modified in the early 1990s to emphasize a bull's eye rash. This rash is not seen by an estimated 50 to 70 percent of persons diagnosed with Lyme.

Another $Lyme trick is to not collect data for Lyme 'in areas not considered to be high risk or endemic for the disease' — thereby ensuring the area will never be categorized as high risk or endemic. This falsely guarantees anyone may cross a county line and enjoy a picnic while sitting on a lovely grassy field and be assured they are not at risk for Lyme until they return to their neighboring Lyme endemic county.

News Flash: *It has been reported that persons crossing into counties which collect no Lyme data have been miraculously cleared of their Lyme infection, as have all the horses, deer, foxes, dogs, cats, birds, little mice and fluffy bunnies!*

The US government's most recent attempt to squelch proof of the Lyme epidemic has been to remove the category from CDC's nationally notifiable diseases Reports, even though Lyme is a nationally notifiable disease.

In 2015, Lyme and other tickborne infections were the sixth most commonly reported diseases in CDC's nationally notifiable disease report. However, there were no cases of Lyme according to the published 2017 and 2018 nationally notifiable disease Reports. *In fact, the category for Lyme has disappeared from these published Reports.*

Theresa Denham, a Lyme advocate and Dream Team member wrote CDC's Acting Director at the Center for Surveillance, Epidemiology and Laboratory Services for clarification. In response to her request asking where one might find the Lyme surveillance data for 2017 and 2018, he recommended Theresa review the same Reports wherein the category for Lyme has been deleted since 2016.

From the Acting Director, *"The data remains available and is consistently updated at https://wwwn.cdc.gov/nndss/ infect-ious-tables.html. You will also find the link to tables for notifiable conditions in the MMWR."*

Many public health authorities in the US, EU, South America, and Asia appear to have made surveillance information regarding Lyme and tickborne diseases less publicly accessible since 2016.

Although there appears to be an overall trend of disappearing Lyme surveillance data, the European Center for Disease Control (ECDC) recently recommended Lyme neuroborreliosis be added to the Europewide surveillance.[23]

The ECDC case definition for Lyme neuroborreliosis in children requires the rather elusive symptoms of the bull's-eye rash and Bell's palsy, plus a confirmation by unreliable Lyme serology tests to qualify.

For adults, cases are confirmed when the person has both white blood cells and antibodies found in CSF. There is ample evidence such criteria will not be met, even when people have neuroborreliosis.

A 2018 equine study of neuroborreliosis found a significant percentage of horses with neuroborreliosis did not test positive for CSF or blood serology tests.[24]

A 2018 human study regarding neuroborreliosis diagnosis recommended both the analysis of anti-*Borrelia* antibodies (serology) simultaneously in blood and in CSF as essential for the accurate diagnosis of neuroborreliosis.[25]

Additionally, EDCD confirmation of neuroborreliosis may include growing the pathogen from patient samples (culture) or a positive direct detection (RNA, DNA) from CSF. These criteria may be difficult to meet.

The 2018 human study (previously cited) stated, 'PCR and DNA sequencing tests may be challenging, since these methods have low sensitivity in CSF and serum specimens'.

$Lyme propaganda has not favored direct detection tests, *because such tests show proof of infection*, whereas positive serology tests can be easily thrown out and dismissed as 'false positive'.

Meanwhile, under the stranglehold of $Lyme, diagnosis is no guarantee for access to adequate treatment. In Sweden, an eight-year-old boy began losing his ability to talk after he twice tested positive for Lyme neuroborreliosis. He was given a short course of antibiotics and his parents were told not to worry about his increasing number of debilitating neurological symptoms.

His deteriorating health had interfered with school attendance and led to more complications for this family. The boy's teachers, neighbors and extended family knew the child had been very ill. His school absentees were automatically reported to central authorities prompting a 'poor parenting' investigation.

There are countless cases across the globe whereby children with confirmed Lyme diagnosis are denied treatment options and parents are investigated because the child's illness causes absenteeism.

*I never give them hell. I just tell the truth
and they think it's hell.*
—Harry S. Truman

Part Three
Some $Lymey Behavior

to be conscious of complete truthfulness while
telling carefully constructed lies, to hold simultaneously
two opinions which cancelled out, to use logic against logic,
to repudiate morality while laying claim to it
—George Orwell, 1984

Chapter 10: How to Manage Truthtellers When Bad Science Cannot be Sold

Number 1: *Call Them Despicable Names ... in Public*

I first met Professor Christian Perronne in 2017 in Geneva. He is a serious-minded and soft-spoken man with a good sense of humor. I have since had the pleasure of meeting his wife and three of his four daughters and can see how his family help keep the world-famous man humble and happy.

Defamation, slandering and libeling by $Lyme Actors has been aggressive and global. The following example of baiting and name-calling of Christian is ludicrous, farcical, harebrained, and cockamamie —and gives new meaning to the word 'absurd'.

Professor Christian Perronne

Christian is a world renown expert in medicine and infectious diseases. He has successfully treated thousands of persons suffering from chronic Lyme and co-infections with extended antimicrobial therapies.

Christian has maintained comprehensive records of these therapies, their effectiveness, and the health status of his patients post treatment.

Christian has held many leadership roles in infectious diseases, tropical diseases, HIV, vaccine development and respiratory illnesses. He has held posts —including director, president, vice president, committee chair— in both highly regarded academic and research centers in France and international bodies. Christian has also founded medical, scientific and advocacy organizations to advance scientific understanding and medical care.

His extensive list of credentials includes: Professor of Infectious and Tropical Diseases at the Faculty of Medicine Paris-Ile de France-Ouest, University of Versailles-St Quentin en Yvelines (Paris); Chief of the Department of Medicine at the Raymond Poincaré University Hospital (Garches) and member of their research unit for biostatistics biomathematics pharma-coepidemiology and infectious diseases; Vice-President of the French federation against tickborne diseases and President of their scientific committee; former Vice-chairman of the National Reference Centre on Tuberculosis and Mycobacteria at the Pasteur Institute in Paris; and past President of the French College of Professors of Infectious and Tropical Diseases.

Christian is also Co-founder and past-President of the French Federation of Infectiology; President of the French National Technical Advisory Group of Experts on Immunization; Chairman at the French Drug Agency's working group making national evidence-based Guidelines for the antibiotic treatment of respiratory tract infections; Principal investigator of several major clinical trials on HIV, mycobacteria and viral hepatitis, for the national agency for research on AIDS; President of the Communicable diseases section at the Conseil Supérieur d'Hygiène Publique de France and then of the Communicable diseases commission at the High Council for Public Health; Member of the scientific committee of the French Institute of Research in Microbiology and Infectious Diseases; President of the National Council of Universities, subsection Infectious and Tropical Diseases; Member and co-chair of the European Advisory Group of Experts on Immunization (ETAGE) at WHO; and an author or co-author of more than 300 scientific publications.

Christian has been the driving force behind the French government's new national plan for tickborne diseases. As of September 16, 2018, the French plan is the most advanced and realistic government strategy for addressing this epidemic among all standing government plans across the globe.

The French plan allows General Practitioners (GP) to provide one month of antibiotic treatment to Lyme patients, even when the Lyme serology is negative. The plan emphasizes the need to treat symptomatic pregnant women, even when they are seronegative.

Furthermore, if the GP determines it necessary to prolong treatment, the GP may then collaborate with an 'expert center' to decide on therapy for persistent infection. The French authorities require the GP to document these treatment regimens, clinical response and the long-term health status of the patient. This information will be collected into databases and used for research protocols.

The French plan does not recognize PTLD$ and addresses some foolish thinking promoted by certain $Lyme Actors to maintain the status quo. The French plan states,

'It is necessary to abstain from the false dichotomy of 'psychosomatic OR biological/organic pathologies ... A practitioner who does not know how to treat his [Lyme, tickborne diseases] patient cannot use therapies for psycho-somatic illness instead of treatment for biological/organic illness and infection.

However, treatment for the psychological distress caused by such infections, as well as psychiatric conditions arising from neurological damage from the infections, may be used in addition to antimicrobial treatments for the infections and biological illness.

Such psychological or psychiatric therapies may only take place if there is a finding they would be useful and after the patient undergoes a thorough assessment by specialists [psychiatrists and neurologists].'

In 2016, Christian gained an *additional title of distinction* when he gave a plenary presentation at the National Academy of Medicine in France.

Christian's presentation was well attended. The balcony was packed full of journalists, Lyme patients and Lyme doctors. The Academicians sat in the main floor area. Among those in the audience was infectious disease specialist and former President of the Academy, Professor Marc Gentilini (retired).

Christian's presentation demonstrated the poor reliability of the standard Lyme serology tests, the persistence of infection and frequency of co-infections. Christian described the many flaws and biases in most of the studies done to evaluate Lyme treatments. His presentation included a formidable number of published references.

Questions were taken from the audience following Christian's presentation. Gentilini, however, gave orders instead of questions. He began his comments with, *"I order you to retract immediately"* and went on to say Christian had given *"an irrational talk"*.

Then, before many hundreds of witnesses and media representatives ...

... Gentilini accused Christian of being a TERRORIST!

These demands and accusations were followed by loud boos from the balcony. Christian calmly and firmly answered Gentilini's charges. His responses were met with loud applause while Gentilini's face went pale.

Number 2:   *Silence Their Voices, Then Fire Them*

The following is another true story, this time set in Norway. My research into $Lyme uncovered similar situations spanning many nations. Threats, sanctions, restrictions and loss of livelihoods have been repeatedly employed to suppress science which counters $Lyme propaganda and dominance.

Professor Morten Laane

For decades, Norwegian microbiology Professor Morten Laane enjoyed the respect of his peers and students as he worked to better understand pathogens at the University of Bergen in Norway. Over time, the Lyme pathogen captivated Morten's interest.

There are different types of diagnostic methods to identify infectious agents. The reproduction of live organisms (or culture) from patient samples is normally the gold standard. Not all pathogens can be cultured.

For more than a century, scientists have tried to culture the bacteria which causes syphilis, with no success. At the time Morten was trying to detect Lyme, microscopy was considered the gold standard in diagnostics for syphilis. Both syphilis and Lyme are in the same 'pathogen family' and scientists and medical experts consider them to be 'cousins'.

Morten set out to find a method to detect the Lyme bacteria in blood —and he succeeded. In 2013, following his research, Morten and a colleague published, <u>A simple method for the detection of live *Borrelia* spirochetes in human blood using classical microscopy techniques</u>. [26] This detection method allowed patients to be diagnosed and treated according to evidence of infection—regardless of prior antibiotic treatment.

Morten was asked to present his paper at a scientific conference. The University may have been pressured by $Lyme because the University threatened to fire Morten should he speak at the conference.

Morten honored the restrictions made by his University—he nevertheless share his discovery by using nonverbal and visual communications. The University then fired Morten and closed his laboratory. His published article disappeared from the scientific journal but has been maintained intact with proof of its publication. [27]

Number 3: *Show Ass to Cover Ass*

It appears some $Lyme professionals may be willing to show their ass in order to cover their ass.

Dr. Johan Bakken

Professor Åse Bengaard Andersen, Chairman of the Danish Society for Infectious Medicine opened an international conference for Lyme medical training on October 26, 2011. Conference attendees included representatives from Germany, Sweden, the US and Denmark. Nine of the 10 conference presentations were focused on scientific and medical information.

That afternoon, former IDSA President, Dr. Johan Bakken presented on 'Scientific evidence and political consequences following the 2006 IDSA Lyme Guidelines.[28] Johan's present-ation had little content suitable for medical training. His presentation largely focused on ILADS, the IDSA competitor for the treatment of Lyme and other tickborne diseases.

Johan's presentation included many false, defamatory and libelous statements against ILADS. Before an international medical and scientific audience, Johan announced,

"ILADS members have resorted to harassment and death threats" —and cited a publication which provided no proof for his outlandish statements.

What would compel a medical professional to make such claims? Could it be that $Lyme has no medical and scientific proof to defend the IDSA Guidelines?

Dr. Art Weinstein

Dr. Art Weinstein made unusual use of his May 2017 class reunion at the University of Toronto. In his presentation to his classmates, Art made many false, derogatory and slanderous statements against Lyme patients, advocates and the doctors who treat persistent cases. He even showed pictures of skeletons wearing 'Lyme awareness' T-shirts.

Like Johan, he provided no proof for his bizarre statements.

Art is a US based rheumatologist with long ties to IDSA. Weinstein was exposed for conflicts of interests while serving as a consultant to the IDSA Panel during the development of the 2006 Lyme Disease Guidelines.

Let's hope his classmates enjoyed the show!

Number 4: *Reward Bad Behavior*

The characteristics of $Lyme Actors include impunity and entitlement. It is not uncommon for $Lymeballs to be barely scolded for grievous actions and judgment. Their actions often result in promotions and financial rewards based upon questionable merits and credentials.

Their main job appears to be denying Lyme diagnosis and treatment and attacking those who treat persons with complicated and persistent cases. They consult as highly paid experts in medical and legal cases to deny diagnosis and treatment and remove licenses of doctors using Lyme treatment Guidelines which meet international standards.

Many in the world of $Lyme academia regurgitate $Lyme literature reviews citing previous literature reviews. They bandy about the long list of recycled propaganda as proof of $Lyme science.

Below is just one of many global examples of impunity and entitlement.

Dr. James Calvert Supports $Lyme
While under on probation for patient death-by-negligence, the Oregon Medical Board fully reinstated James' license prior to his beginning the required remediation program. Following his reinstatement, James then became an employee of Oregon Health Authority as Director of the Southern Oregon Community Care Organization (CCO).

CCOs implement the Oregon Health Plan for low-income patients. As Director, James has obstructed access to Lyme diagnosis and treatment for many, including a severely ill child from a low-income family. This child had a documented history of tick bites, positive Lyme serology tests, and symptoms of Lyme arthritis. The child went on to develop life threatening cardiac complications, as well as serious and observable neurological complications. The parents appealed to James for the child's access to Lyme treatment. James responded by securing a neurologist who stated the child's lab tests were 'false positive'.

As of March 2017, James enjoys an influential advisory role for the Oregon Department of Health. He is called upon to testify against doctors who treat persons with persistent and complicated cases of Lyme and Lyme-like illness.

Number 5: *Threaten to Take Away their Children, Then Pay Someone to Take Away Their Children*

Almost every week, I receive correspondence from desperate parents across the globe asking me what can be done to keep the government from taking away their children who are under treatment for Lyme. These parents have come to the attention of the authorities for many different reasons.

Sometimes investigations are triggered by children's school absenteeism. Other times investigations are triggered by parents' outspoken advocacy and criticism of failed government policies for the Lyme epidemic. I have been asked to provide expert testimony in legal cases in the US on this matter.

In the Netherlands, Canada, the US, France, the UK and many other nations, the parents of children suffering from complicated cases of Lyme are accused of 'Munchausen by proxy'. Munchausen by proxy is a mental illness whereby a person falsifies illness in another.

Some governments pay a private intermediary organization to manage their caseloads for child protective services. Some of these organizations are awarded money for every child taken from their parents. Such organizations have a strong financial incentive to seize children from their families; the children are then denied medical care for Lyme. There are Reports from many nations of seized children put into psychiatric care and forced to take psychotropic drugs.

An independent Dutch child advocacy organization, known as BVIKZ, began to investigate false claims of child neglect and abuse by the Dutch Child Protection Services. By March 2017, they had investigated 168 individual cases, of which more than thirty percent involved children being treated for Lyme.

Unfortunately, the Dutch government has been suckered into believing the $Lyme PTLD$ fraud. Any child treated for Lyme and unable to attend school following a short course of antibiotics is determined to have a psychosomatic illness or to be the victim of bad parents. In these cases, the severity of their illness caused the children to miss school for extended periods of time. Schools are being used to perpetuate these abuses.

Research indicates that less than one percent of the population may suffer from Munchausen by proxy, a condition which is very hard to prove. Dutch TV news exposed how the intermediary organization fraudulently mislabeled most of the parents with sick children who miss school with Munchausen by proxy. This organization is paid by the Dutch government.

Number 6: *When All Else Fails, KILL!*

Tabitha: There is Something Rotten in Denmark

The Danish government aggressively promotes the IDSA Lyme Guidelines, the standard Lyme serology tests and suppresses dissenting scientific views and practices.

The government sponsored a documentary called 'Cheating or *Borrelia*' produced by TV2. The documentary defamed the Danish Lyme patient group and the laboratories and practitioners who have helped this patient group obtain diagnosis and treatment.

The Danish government and their documentary inflicted grave and injurious harm against Tabitha Nielsen. Tabitha was a young mother who had been previously diagnosed with incurable and fatal motor neuron disease.

Tabitha sought additional medical opinions and was diagnosed with Lyme. The Danish health system refused to give her Lyme treatment, so Tabitha started a successful fundraising campaign. Tabitha's health began to improve under Lyme treatment and she became a vocal critic of how the Danish health care system had left her to die instead of treating her Lyme infection.[29]

TV2 staff misled the Lyme patients they interviewed for the documentary. TV2 claimed they would be fair and sympathetic to the situation. Instead, Tabitha's interview and footage were edited in a manner to make her appear pathetic, unrealistic and to be a stooge for anybody who promised to improve her health.

The government's $Lyme propaganda was effective. Following the documentary, her supporters withdrew their financial assistance. Without access to treatment, Tabitha's health swiftly deteriorated. The Danish authorities have told Tabitha her future hospital care will be limited to a ventilator and limited palliative care.

Shortly after the documentary was aired, it was discovered the TV2 executives were earning nearly double the salary of the executives in private TV networks in Denmark.

$Lyme propaganda pays well —and kills.

Teike: Euthanasia Instead of Generic Antibiotics

In many countries, euthanasia is an option for those suffering from fatal diseases which cause unbearable suffering. The 2002 Dutch Law 'Termination of Life on Request and Assisted Suicide Act' states euthanasia must be undertaken in accordance with criteria of due care, such as *'the absence of reasonable alternatives to address the patient's unbearable and hopeless suffering'*.

Prior to being bitten by a tick, Teike Van Baden was a healthy young man with a fulfilling life. He enjoyed challenging work in the music industry, jogging in the morning and an active social life. Teike's tick bite was followed by the typical bull's-eye rash, Bell's palsy and other symptoms which indicated acute Lyme infection. Following the classic Lyme symptoms, he developed severe headaches, light and noise sensitivity, spasms and seizures. Teike then developed additional serious neurological, arthritic and cardiac complications.

Despite sharing information regarding his tick bite and bull's-eye rash, his many trips to medical centers and hospitals resulted in no testing for Lyme. In desperation, Teike sought an expert outside his health plan. Laboratory tests confirmed he had both Lyme and Bartonella infection. Teike responded well to the generic antibiotics but relapsed each time his treatment ended.

In 2017, Teike's medical records showed his quality of life to be quite bearable when he is under antibiotic treatment. Unfortunately, Teike struggles to pay for his treatments. When he explored options with his insurer, Zilveren Kruis, they replied they would not cover medical treatment for his condition, but they would cover the cost of his euthanasia.

Teike received this deadly polite correspondence from his insurer at the age of 29!

I am happy to report Teike is still with us and advocates for advances in Lyme diagnosis and treatment. He has interviewed highly regarded physicians and scientists and written many thoughtful articles on the topic.

*Corruption is authority
plus monopoly
minus transparency.*

PART FOUR
Human Rights Hardball

*I will not let anyone walk through my mind
with their dirty feet.*
— Mahatma Gandhi

Chapter 11: Stealth Required

Back in Florida I estimated the Dream Team had 86 days to meet the March 2017, ICD11 deadline. I began the complicated task of organizing a strategy which would compel WHO to change its codes for Lyme.

I had reviewed the unending slick $Lyme spiral of pseudo-medical tales spun through decades. I knew, in order to make headway, we had to change the framework and the language of how this epidemic is presented to others. The magnitude and treachery of $Lyme demanded all my decades of successful human rights advocacy.

We had to stop limiting ourselves to the medical and scientific debates, because these were controlled by $Lymeballs positioned in most major publishing arenas, many academic centers, private health care companies and many government agencies. We had to call this situation for what it is —decades of human rights violations, orchestrated and implemented by many Actors across the globe.

Therefore, we would not refer to diagnostic testing as a choice between technologies. We had to frame the *deliberate obstruction to the access of diagnostic tests which meet legitimate standards.*

We were not going to debate the pros and cons of various treatment options. We had to frame the *deliberate obstruction to the access of treatment options which meet international standards.* We had to speak the ugly truth of how those who provide medical care to this patient group are *routinely threatened with the loss of their livelihoods.*

We had to expose the *inhumane shameful acts by governments and organizations paid to seize sick children*. We had to show the immorality and indecency in practices whereby *persons, able to manage an illness with generic antimicrobials, were offered euthanasia.*

Most importantly, we had to directly tie all these human rights violations explicitly to the limited ICD10 codes for Lyme.

This required we develop Reports which were comprehensive in nature. These Reports needed to document all medical and scientific evidence to move the ICD agenda and specify every human rights violation associated with this epidemic. The Reports required an elaboration of each and every failure on the part of State Actors with regard to this global public health crisis, as well as their complicity in the related profiteering.

These Reports were only the first step. Top-level political support was needed in short order. We had to gain audience with decision makers responsible for the topics covered in our Reports. The most strategic support for this agenda meant we needed to gain audience with two particular UN Special Rapporteurs. These were the Special Rapporteurs for health human rights and the defenders of human rights.

The only way we could gain audience with Special Rapporteurs was if our written words were so compelling, that among the many thousands of requests they receive, we would gain entry.

As a veteran of UN bureaucratic politics, I knew certain protocols must be followed and every procedure properly completed to be established as credible stakeholders. We also had to meet every requirement in our submissions to WHO. These protocols and procedures involved multiple commun- ications across various WHO divisions as well as the UN Human Rights Council.

We had to wade into an extremely complex digital Beta platform, as well as provide comprehensive documents which built a global rationale for changing the codes. We enlisted the help of graduate students recruited from Canada and Finland to enter many hundreds of data points across the ICD11 system to support our recommendations. Every entry was on standing record for the world to see and was thoroughly documented.

Another challenge our Dream Team had was finding peer-reviewed publications for the many complications of this insidious illness. Unfortunately, $Lyme Actors have had the power to reject many professional publications which counter their propaganda. Our Dream Team could only promote recognition of those complications for which there are solid peer-reviewed publications. This means that although ICD11 is an historic improvement over previous versions, complications which are both common and severely debilitating are still missing from ICD11.

Many peer reviewed publications supported the following conditions were recommended for code assignments:

Congenital Lyme disease, persistent infection, Borrelial lymphocytoma, Granuloma annulare, morphea, localized scleroderma, lichen sclerosis and atrophicus, Lyme meningitis, Lyme nephritis, Lyme hepatitis, Lyme myositis, Lyme aortic aneurysm, coronary artery aneurysm, late Lyme endocarditis, Lyme carditis, Late Lyme neuritis or neuropathy, Meningovascular and Neuroborreliosis —with cerebral infarcts, Intracranial aneurysm, Lyme Parkinsonism, Late Lyme meningoencephalitis or meningomyelo-encephalitis, Atrophic form of Lyme meningoencephalitis with dementia and subacute presenile dementia, Neuropsychiatric manifestations, late Lyme disease of liver and other viscera, late Lyme disease of kidney and ureter, late Lyme disease of Bronchus and lung and Latent Lyme disease, unspecified.

I anticipated our Report to WHO might not be well received, given that $Lyme has its tentacles everywhere. $Lyme, however, would be powerless to erase our entries into the digital platform. Any rejection on the part of WHO regarding our recommendations required publicly presented rationales. Any rejections of our entries were followed by formal inquiries to multiple WHO divisions and on the digital platform.

I contacted many in my international professional network to assist us in this daunting endeavor. As an example, a former US Assistant Secretary of State asked the global health ambassador to petition for meetings with WHO.

This dynamic brew of information, connection, and efforts was bubbling across the globe. Unfortunately, I made the mistake of sharing some of our plans with Lyme advocates whom I regarded as allies. I then discovered they had attempted to undermine our work. The situation required strategic confidentiality and stealth to prevent the advertising of our efforts to $Lyme and their enablers.

My days and nights became a blur of time zones from other countries and tasks regarding research, Report synthesizing, political petitioning and maneuvering and logistical details.

The Dream Team needed to have representatives at key meetings in Geneva, Switzerland. The Dream Team does not use its name for fundraising and so this was an additional challenge. Each member was going to travel on their own dime —*if we secured the meetings.*

Suddenly, things started to break our way —the most important meeting with the Special Rapporteur for health human rights was secured. I was then contacted by Barbara Buchman, the Executive Director of ILADS and asked if we needed financial support for airfare and hotels in Geneva. I could not believe our good fortune and immediately submitted a proposal to the sister organization of ILADS, known as International Lyme and Associated Diseases Education Foundation (ILADEF). ILADEF funded a significant portion of our first trip to Geneva. This enabled Dream Team representatives from Australia, US, Nigeria, the Czech Republic, the Netherlands, France, and Sweden to testify to the Special Rapporteur for health human rights. Representatives from Switzerland also participated as did Canadian representatives, who were funded by Canadian Lyme Foundation.

$Lyme is Featured in Liberia

In between these elaborate machinations, I took an assignment for the US government to Liberia. This required I travel throughout many regions of the country to assess how local government was supporting education, employment, health-care, and other services to marginalized populations, including the disabled.

Between encounters with a deadly green mamba snake in one office and a giant scorpion in my rural hotel room, I met an incredible number of inspiring and resilient Liberians com-mitted to advancing their nation.

As part of my assignment, I provided case studies on corrupt-ion for my counterparts to work through and remediate.

Guess what?

$Lyme was well featured in these case studies and there are now many Liberians who know about this corruption in the US and the global health care sector.

While in Liberia, I had the good fortune to meet a senior official with the US Department of Health and Human Services (HHS) who was about to retire. He was very candid with me regarding $Lyme and said, *'they are not going to be able to keep covering up the truth for much longer.'* He also encouraged me to push forward.

Upon my return from Liberia, and prior to my departure for Geneva, I assembled all the human rights violations against persons living with Lyme and Lyme-like illness, as well as the their human rights defenders. Their human rights defenders include medical professionals who provide their care, as well as the parents who try to protect their children's rights to life, medical care and bodily integrity.

The following list was also provided as part of a public comment registered for US federal Tickborne Disease Working Group; it has never been posted by HHS.

Human Rights Hardball

The many egregious practices related to the 2006 IDSA Lyme Guidelines have perpetrated fourteen human rights violations across the globe and are detailed in eleven human rights treatises.

Such treatises and other international documents are relevant to international human rights law and the protection of human rights. Treatises are ratified and signed by nations which support these human rights and can be used to enforce protections of human rights.

Human rights are based on the principle of respect for the individual. Their fundamental assumption is each person deserves to be treated with dignity and these rights are universal.

The recognition of human rights evolved over centuries. In response to the devastations of World War II, the Member States of the newly formed United Nations assembled and codified the thirty Articles of human rights. These rights have been universally promoted and many of these rights are today part of the constitutional laws of democratic nations.

The IDSA views on Lyme are mirrored in the inaccurate presentation of Lyme in ICD and result in millions being obstructed from diagnosis and treatment, The codes have perpetuated an inadequate response to an epidemic expanding in all world regions.

Lyme borreliosis is the only known infectious disease whereby licensed practitioners treating patients according to Guidelines which meet internationally accepted standards are constantly at risk for the loss of their licenses and livelihoods.

These human rights violations are detailed in the Report The Situation of Human Rights Defenders of Lyme and Relapsing Fever Borreliosis Patients: Edition One and have been entered into record by Special Rapporteurs with the UN Human Rights Council.

Applicable Human Rights[30]

The pertinent human rights of Lyme and relapsing fever patients and their human rights defenders are found in the following international and regional treatises:

African Charter on Human and Peoples' Rights
Convention Against Torture
European Convention for the Prevention of Torture and Inhuman or Degrading Treatment or Punishment
Convention on the Elimination of All Forms of Discrimination against Women
Convention on the Rights of the Child
Convention on the Rights of Persons with Disabilities
European Convention on the Protection of Human Rights and Fundamental Freedoms
European Social Charter
International Covenant on Civil and Political Rights
International Covenant on Economic, Social, and Cultural Rights —Article 12 states steps for the realization of the right to health include those which:
- reduce infant mortality and ensure the healthy development of the child
- improve environmental and industrial hygiene
- prevent, treat and control epidemic, endemic, occupational and other diseases
- create conditions to ensure access to health care for all.
International Convention on the Elimination of All Forms of Racial Discrimination

In addition, internationally ratified standards now stipulate:

The right to liberty and security of the person has been held to prohibit unauthorized disclosure of personal health data.

The right to bodily integrity and security of the person have been held to prohibit the administration of medicine to a child against parents' wishes.

The right to freedom from cruel, inhuman, or degrading treatment or punishment has been held to oblige governments to secure the adequate health and well-being of prisoners.

The right to bodily integrity is interpreted to be part of the right to security of the person, the right to freedom from torture and cruel, inhuman, and degrading treatment, and the right to the highest attainable standard of health.

The right to health includes the human rights in patient care as well as economic and political human rights which define the context of patient care provided by human rights defenders.

The situation of borreliosis patients and their defenders show fourteen violations across eleven human rights treatises.

Human Rights Violations of Patients and their Human Rights Defenders

Right to highest attainable standard of health
State health authorities allow insurers and state programs for low income families to deny medical care for Lyme and Lyme-like illness.

These policies result in obstruction to necessary medical care for those with insufficient economic resources to pay out-of-pocket for their medical care.

Patients who are limited to programs for low income families are given inferior care.

Right to freedom from torture and cruel, inhuman and degrading treatment
State policies restricting antibiotic access for the Lyme and Lyme-like illnesses cause patients to suffer unnecessary pain, disability, bankruptcy, and even death.

State Actors cause doctors mental and emotional anguish when they are forced to abandon their patients or are barred from applying clinical practice Guidelines which have been vetted through internationally accepted standards. This results in patients suffering unnecessary pain, disability, bankruptcy, and even death.

Right to life
Outdated and politicized State Lyme policies result in disability, bankruptcy and suicide for many Lyme patients.

Right to liberty and security of person
Lyme patients are forced into psychiatric care for wrongful diagnoses of psychosomatic and psychiatric illness and are denied medical care for persistent infection.

Right to privacy and confidentiality
Lyme patients' medical information is shared without their consent to State authorities who harass their doctors for providing Lyme treatment options which meet internationally accepted standards.

Right to information
The State fails to provide information regarding the risk of disability and death from undiagnosed and inadequately treated Lyme.

The State routinely misinforms the public regarding the reliability of the diagnostic serology tests and increases their risk from disability and death from undiagnosed Lyme.

Practitioners fail to provide Lyme patients with information about treatment options and the potential risks and benefits of these options versus lack of treatment.

Right to bodily integrity
Practitioners fail to obtain free and informed consent from patients before treatments begin.

Threats of loss of license and livelihood against doctors who treat Lyme patients according to protocols which have met internationally accepted standards results in many doctors turning away Lyme patients, leading to patient suicides and death.

Right to participation in public policy
State Actors fund grantees and other affiliates to disseminate articles which recommend Lyme patients and their human rights defenders be excluded from participating in Lyme-related policies.

Participation in Lyme-related public policy by Lyme patients and their human rights defenders is 'empty theater' with no evidence of political commitment to change status quo and prioritize patient care. As an example, State Actors collude for wrongful financial incentives to drive preplanned outcomes which suppress science and maintain status quo.

Right to nondiscrimination and equality
Medical practitioners, hospitals and policymakers are encouraged to claim Lyme patients have psychosomatic issues rather than biological illness, resulting in obstruction to medical care for infection and complications.

Right to decent working conditions
Clinical practice Guidelines of a professional medical society meeting internationally accepted standards and its members are defamed, harassed and threatened by State Actors who belong to a competing private medical society and their affiliates.

Right to freedom of association
Authorities use penalties to prevent practitioners who use Guidelines which meet internationally accepted standards to travel to conferences.

Authorities prevent scientists from providing presentations promoting diagnostics tests which compete with the authorities' (and their affiliates') patented tests.

Right to due process
A practitioner facing disciplinary proceedings is denied access to all evidence presented against him/her in advance of the hearing.

A doctor in a medical judgment suit is put on strict limitations and has not given a 'hearing' date two years after the commencement of the proceedings.

Right to a remedy
The State takes no action to address any of the violations described above.

Truth is incontrovertible,
malice may attack it and ignorance may deride it,
but, in the end, there it is.
—Sir Winston Churchill

PART FIVE
ICD11 Whup Ass

Lying is a delightful thing for it leads to the truth.
—Fyodor Dostoevsky

Chapter 12: Easy to diagnose, treat and cure' Repudiated by ICD11

$Lymeball Breached

In June 2018, Lada Zavadilová, a veterinarian from the Czech Republic and member of our international Dream Team, alerted me to the fact WHO had released the draft ICD11. I quickly went to the WHO's globally accessible digital platform and found radically improved ICD11 codes for Lyme!

These new ICD11 codes for Lyme reveal that indeed, there have been decades of harmful $Lyme propaganda corrupting Lyme policies and Guidelines across many nations.

Furthermore, the groundbreaking changes demonstrated our strategy to link human rights violations and corruption to the ICD codes had broken through the decades of 'controlled medical debate' and changed the conversation.

The Special Rapporteurs and other UN officials paid close attention to our presentations on how the codes for Lyme and the IDSA Lyme Guidelines were corrupted and destroying lives.

I was very moved to hear Dr. Kenneth Liegner, after 40 years of advocacy, testify before an official audience who cares about such abuses. Ken spoke of his prior collaboration with CDC. Ken's patient Vicki Logan had tested negative by multiple serology tests; these are the same tests recommended by CDC and IDSA. CDC then identified the Lyme pathogen in the CSF of his patient. These pathogens were found after multiple prior antibiotic treatments. Early on, Vicki's private health insurer covered extended intravenous antibiotic treatment which improved her condition. Later, when in a nursing home and under Medicaid, her intravenous antibiotic treatment was suspended.

While Ken sought mechanisms for Medicaid reimbursement, Vicki experienced grand mal seizures and was transferred to a local hospital where Ken did not have privileges. There Vicki was found to have low blood pressure. Her condition was not investigated, and her family was persuaded to support a 'do not resuscitate' order. She subsequently died.

An autopsy revealed ongoing neurologic Lyme infection and an acute heart attack which was neither diagnosed nor treated. [31] This was an unconscionable case of medical execution of a middle-aged woman who experienced quality of life while under treatment for Lyme infection.

The ICD11 debunks $Lyme's decades of denial and dismissal of the epidemic and those living with the illness. Lyme as portrayed in ICD11 does not resemble an infection which is 'easy diagnose, treat and cure'.

The disease presented in the ICD11 specifically recognizes Vicki's life threatening Lyme complications.

The New Global Face of Lyme

ICD10 Codes for Lyme borreliosis were limited to:

A69.2	Lyme Disease
M01.2	Arthritis due to Lyme
G01	Meningitis due to Lyme
G63.0	Polyneuropathy due to Lyme

ICD11 is far more comprehensive than ICD10, however, many complications from Lyme still require codes.

ICD11

1C1G	Lyme borreliosis
1C1G.0	Early cutaneous Lyme borreliosis
1C1G.1	Disseminated Lyme borreliosis
1C1G.10	Lyme Neuroborreliosis
1C1G.11	Lyme Carditis
1C1G.12	Ophthalmic Lyme borreliosis
1C1G.13	Lyme arthritis
1C1G.14	Late cutaneous Lyme borreliosis
1C1G.1Y	Other specified disseminated Lyme borreliosis
1C1G.1Z	Disseminated Lyme borreliosis, unspecified
1C1G.2	Congenital Lyme borreliosis
1C1GY	Other specified Lyme borreliosis
6D85.Y	Dementia due to other specified diseases classified elsewhere; Dementia due to Lyme Disease
9C20.1	Infectious panuveitis; Infectious panuveitis in Lyme disease
9B66.1	Infectious intermediate Chorioditis; Infectious intermediate uveitis in Lyme disease
8A45.0Y	Other Specified white matter disorders due to infections; Central Nervous System demyelination due to Lyme borreliosis

ICD11 now recognizes fifteen complications from Lyme borreliosis whereas the ICD10 recognized three complications from the disease.

The Lyme case definition emphasizes arthritis as the signifying complication and ignores many life threatening outcomes. In contrast, of the fifteen new codes, six describe infection in the central nervous system.

The ICD11 demonstrates and confirms Lyme has affinity for 'immune privileged sites' such as the central nervous system.

Five of the fifteen codes identify complications documented as life threatening: Lyme Neuroborreliosis, Lyme Carditis, Congenital Lyme borreliosis, Dementia due to Lyme Disease, and Central Nervous System demyelination due to Lyme borreliosis.

ICD11 codes for Lyme now describe a disease which may cause severe and potentially fatal central nervous system complications and is passed from pregnant mother to fetus.

Many of the new codes describe late stage and systemic complications. These codes demonstrate the infection is not easy to diagnose.

Fourteen of the fifteen ICD11 codes can be applied to late stage and persistent forms of the illness.

The codes underscore the unreliability of the recommended serology diagnostics —meaning they do not capture infection. Recommended serology diagnostic tests have an approximate reliability of 50 percent for males and only 40 percent for females. There are many pathogenic species and strains belonging to Lyme bacteria found throughout the globe. There are no diagnostic tests for many species and strains of *Borrelia*.

The multiple codes for late stage and systemic complications also demonstrate widespread treatment failure following the standard short-term antibiotics. There is treatment failure for 20 percent in the acute phase of the disease. Approximately 36 percent of all Lyme patients treated with short-term antibiotics develop long-term complications suggesting persistence infection.

The need for multiple codes for late stage and systemic complications prove the infection is not easy to treat nor cure.

According to CDC's website, '*patients who have symptoms like fatigue, pain and joint and muscle aches after the treatment of Lyme disease have posttreatment Lyme disease syndrome (PTLDS) or post Lyme disease syndrome (PLDS)*'.

Guess what? Neither PTLD$ nor PLDS is recognized in ICD11, nor were these syndromes recognized in the previous versions of the ICD. Why won't you find PTLD$ in the ICD11? Because this syndrome has never been validated as a diagnosis.

Furthermore, the theoretical basis for this syndrome is a psychosomatic condition which has been repudiated by the American Psychiatric Association and deleted from their guidance.

The terms PTLD$ and PLDS are the darlings of $Lymeballs thrilled to deny the epidemic and withhold medical care from those living with persistent illness.

Now that $Lyme propaganda has been repudiated, how does one describe the new global face of Lyme? There is encouraging research underway which may provide more effective treatment. The following summary is based upon the science supporting ICD11 Lyme codes.

SUMMARY

In many cases, Lyme is hard to diagnose, treat and cure.

Lyme is a disease known to be transmitted by ticks to humans and from mother to fetus.

Any person who interacts with nature is at risk for exposure and infection. Children are in the high risk category. Adults and children who engage in any outdoor activity without wearing protective gear and repellent appear to have the greatest risk for exposure and infection.

The Borrelia pathogens which cause Lyme and Lyme-like illness are found throughout the globe. There are no diagnostic tests for many species and strains of Borrelia.

Lyme is hard to diagnose unless practitioners are properly trained to undertake clinical and differential diagnosis, and until direct detection diagnostics are made available. Most of the early symptoms of the illness are common to many other illnesses, often making early diagnosis difficult.

Some symptoms of acute Lyme infection may be a bull's-eye rash, Bell's palsy or swelling of the joints; however, many infected persons do not show these symptoms.

Lyme is hard to treat successfully with antimicrobials unless the individual case has been diagnosed prior to entrenched dissemination and immunosuppression. Patients may need repeated treatments to manage the infection, address co-infections and other therapies to improve immune function.

Undiagnosed, untreated or inadequately treated pregnant women can suffer miscarriage.

Lyme can be congenitally transmitted; an infected fetus may have severe and life threatening developmental abnormalities and die.

Undiagnosed, untreated or inadequately treated Lyme may cause potentially fatal complications of the heart, brain and/or nervous system.

Other complications from Lyme include immunosuppression, disabling fatigue, cognitive issues, the dysregulation of any bodily system and organ compromise and failure.

To date, it appears persons with early diagnosis and immediate antimicrobial therapy have less complications from this infection; however, it is unknown if they are cleared of the infection.

For reasons still to be determined, there is a wide range of response to antimicrobial treatment options. The percentage of persons who go in and out of remission, or develop ongoing sequela is estimated at least 36 percent.

ICD11 gives procedural instruction on adding complications to the Lyme code. A following preview shows a sampling of additional codes which can be added to a Lyme diagnosis (there are more in the ICD11). A well-informed medical practitioner can find many combinations to describe multiple complications from this illness.

Post coordination: Add detail to Lyme borreliosis; Use additional code, if desired, examples are:
1D00.0 Bacterial encephalitis
1D01.0 Bacterial meningitis
1D02.0 Bacterial myelitis
BC42.1 Infectious myocarditis
8B88.0 Bell's palsy
9A10.0 Infections of the lacrimal gland
9C20.2 Purulent endophthalmitis

WHO ICD Code Process

Implementation of ICD11 is set to begin following endorsement at the Seventy-second World Health Assembly in May 2019. Rollout will begin immediately, however, member states have until January 1, 2022 to have fully operational ICD11 in place.

ICD11 represents a multiyear and multi-stakeholder process. All 193 countries making up the United Nations were invited to participate and most engaged through numerous venues convened and implemented by the WHO and WHO Collaborating Centers from each region of the world.

Stakeholders engagement included both government and civil society. Government officials from medical, scientific, financial and military agencies, scientific and medical experts from academia and private sector, a wide range of healthcare providers and healthcare practitioners, patient groups, family caregivers, and the insurance and pharmaceutical industries were all represented and through multiple stakeholder events.

At the October 2016 Tokyo, Japan ICD11 Revision Conference, the former Director General of WHO, Dr. Margaret Chan said, *"This has been the most challenging, complex, and far-reaching ICD revision in the 100-year history of this standard statistical instrument."*

More than 450 individuals and institutions from around the world attended the ICD11 Revision Conference in Tokyo, Japan. The countries represented at this one venue alone included: Albania, Algeria, Argentina, Australia, Brazil, Cambodia, Canada, China, Denmark, Egypt, Ethiopia, Finland, India, Indonesia, Iran, Japan, Kenya, Korea, Kuwait, Malaysia, Mexico, Mozambique, Myanmar, Namibia, Nepal, the Netherlands, the Philippines, Republic of Korea, Russian Federation, Rwanda, Slovakia, Sri Lanka, Sweden, Tanzania, Thailand, Turkmenistan, Uganda, UK and the US.

The ICD11 revision includes 10,000 suggested revisions, multiple expert group reviews across the globe and 31 countries undertook test implementation of the new ICD11 codes before the June 2018 release. The ICD11 is the first version which will have the capacity for continuous updating ICD11. These new processes are being determined.

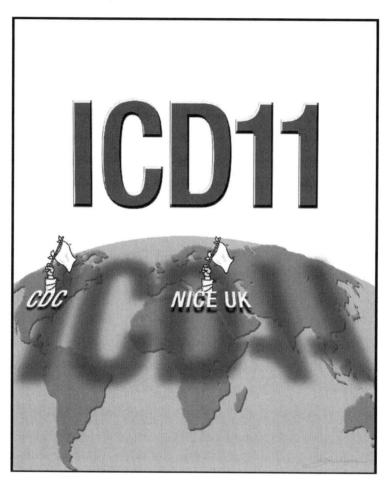

*There is no more neutrality in the world. You either have to
be part of the solution, or you're going
to be part of the problem.*
—Eldridge Cleaver

Chapter 13: $Lyme Response to ICD11
—Dead Silence

Under the circumstances, what are they going to say?

The World Health Organization is a unique entity. WHO is the only global and intergovernmental body dedicated to public health. WHO is not a perfect organization, however, it commands global respect and every government is represented in WHO.

WHO implements strict standards for transparency and accountability requiring inclusiveness and adherence to best practices for scientific and medical review. Every new ICD code for Lyme was substantiated by multiple peer-reviewed medical and scientific publications written by experts from any and all nations. The new codes validate the science demonstrating the persistence and severity of this illness, and the many publications which have been actively suppressed and excluded by $Lyme.

Many of these publications represent primary research on topics which have been blocked from grant support by $Lyme Actors. As an example, much of the primary research on congenital Lyme was completed before the mid-1990s. This research showed the infection causes miscarriage, severe developmental abnormalities of the fetus and fetal death.

Professor Garth Erhlich of Drexel University in Pennsylvania was one of the few courageous souls to go on public record regarding unethical grant denial practices against those researching the chronic forms of the disease.

$Lyme Actors have deliberately and systematically excluded most of this science and medical documentation from most national Lyme Guidelines and policy processes.

In 2017 and 2018, the governments of Canada and the United Kingdom deliberately biased Lyme Guidelines development by excluding preeminent and primary research on Lyme 'because it was not authored by one of their country's citizens or did not study their citizens' or because the primary research, happened prior to an arbitrary date.

The *Borrelia* pathogens which cause Lyme and Lyme-like illness do not differentiate between nationalities. The absurdity of excluding studies 'based on population' —particularly the multiethnic and multiracial populations found in both Canada and the UK— is an astounding act of impunity against the norms of medical and scientific review.

In addition to excluding and suppressing sound science, other tactics have been used to maintain $Lyme dominance. These Canadian, UK and US processes routinely flout the laws, regulations and well-founded norms regarding transparency, accountability and stakeholder representation. In every case, critical and central questions were ignored, and stakeholder representation was reduced to theater.

US Federal Tickborne Diseases Working Group

The US federal Tickborne Diseases Working Group (Working Group), employed similar techniques in 2017 and 2018. The Working Group's draft Report to Congress promotes the status quo. The Report indicates persons suffering from persistent and complicated Lyme may simply have a trivial psychosomatic condition. The Report explicitly states the Working Group has 'no opinion' on this medical fraud or how doctors who treat those suffering from persistent Lyme have been attacked.

[Working Group Report to Congress, page 63] *"Physicians who choose to follow the ILADS Guidelines are often criticized by other physicians and penalized by state medical boards, causing many providers to avoid treating chronically ill patients."*

[page 75] *"Physicians cannot even agree on what to call the illness: Some call it chronic Lyme disease; others call it posttreatment Lyme disease syndrome; and still others claim the illness "is all in their patients' heads." ... This Report does not represent a particular stance on these issues."*

In fact, this stance by the Working Group is not neutral; this signifies the capture of the Working Group by $Lyme. This stance support $Lyme status quo.

[page 82] *"We ... pledge to be transparent in all of our proceedings and to honor our commitments to ourselves and others ... "*

As of September 18, 2018, the Working Group has posted less than five percent of the public comments received. Furthermore, one of their subcommittees canceled the scheduled ICD code presentation with no reason offered. Federal and contractor staff supporting the Working Group stated they had received the human rights comments in time for public posting. All public comments regarding human rights violations have been excluded from public viewing.

Federal advisory committees are required to make available minutes and videos of their public meetings. As of September 18, 2018, the Working Group has failed in their duty to post minutes of the majority of public meetings. Their promised videos of the meetings remain archived and inaccessible to the public. These acts violate of routine transparency practices of federal advisory committees.

The public is denied access to shameful and revealing moments, such as the Working Group response to the Bruzzese family. During the May 15-16, 2018 Public meeting, a subcommittee recommended new laws to protect persons suffering from persistent and complicated Lyme. Julia Bruzzese's father then detailed the clear violations of the Americans With Disabilities Act regarding Julia being denied treatment for Lyme and other tickborne illnesses. Six members of the Bruzzese family then testified to the human rights abuse experienced by Julia.

Following the testimonials, members of the Working Group said the Americans With Disabilities Act was sufficient to protect persons disabled by Lyme. The Working Group then edited out language from the subcommittee's recommendations which detailed specific protections for persons suffering from persistent and complicated Lyme. The Working Group determined these revised recommendations did not require Congressional attention in 2018.

$Lyme is characterized by both scientific and medical fraud, along with opportunistic and predatory financial profiteering and routine acts of misrepresentation.

The Working Group's legal charter requires seven federal members, and Vice Chair Kristen Honey claims to be one of the required seven federal members. Kristen is an employee of Stanford University. The Working Group does not appear to meet the requirements of its legal charter.

Over a period of approximately six months, Kristen claimed to be a federal employee while being an employee of Stanford

University. Kristen simultaneously promoted the brand named *Lyme Innovation* to market both the Working Group and her personal patent which claims 'to cure Lyme' .

[page 82 Report to Congress] *"We are honest, civil, and ethical in our conduct, speech, and interactions with our colleagues and collaborators. We expect our people ... [to] not manipulate facts and data to a particular end or agenda."*

Vice Chair Kristen offered a position to an advocate and asked the advocate to recruit recognized Lyme leaders to support Kristen and an 'undisclosed' project. Apart from the position offered, it appears other incentives were offered to entice several other advocates to support Kristen.

There appears to be considerable efforts made to protect the Working Group; advocates were apparently recruited to silence those who criticize the Working Group's IDSA bias and lack of transparency. There were falsehoods and personal attacks against selected advocates disseminated across multiple institutions

The Working Group is currently promoting Centers of Excellence (Centers) to research and treat Lyme. Public discussions of these proposed Centers make no commitment to consider affordability or accessibility for patients.

Verbal descriptions of the Centers by members of the Working Group detail establishments for those with 'chronic illness' and do not prioritize Lyme patients. Descriptions of the Centers include a four-hour initial patient assessment and the promotion of certain therapies and practices, which few, if any, insurers will cover.

These and other statements indicate the Centers of Excellence will be limiting access to those who can pay out-of-pocket and perhaps be profit centers for those affiliated with the Working Group.

Lyme Advocacy Groups

The globally disseminated information regarding the ground-breaking Lyme ICD11 codes has been roundly ignored by $Lyme allies. There appears to be intentional disregard of this information by certain Lyme nonprofits.

There are many fake or compromised patient advocacy organizations in different disease groups. They are commonly found in 'big-ticket medical cost' diseases, where profit streams are being protected. These Astroturf organizations include fake patient groups for Alzheimer's and MS. They are almost entirely funded by a pharmaceutical industry intent upon maintaining or building their market share of clients.

$Lyme infiltrates or influences patient organizations as well. Across the globe there are substantial, well-financed non-profits and charities which claim to represent those living with Lyme and tickborne illnesses.

Transparency regarding funding practices for nonprofit organizations is not only considered ethical practice, it is required by law. After all, most people want to know who is funding an organization and where the money is going. Honorable nonprofits and charities routinely provide more funding information than that which is required by law.

According to the National Council of Nonprofits, *"Leaders of charitable nonprofits know that financial transparency will help preserve the very-important trust each donor places in a nonprofit with each contribution ... Earning trust through financial transparency and accountability goes beyond what the law requires ..."* Most sound non-profits adopt and post a conflict of interest policy and other financial information on the nonprofit's website, such as a copy of the organization's recent IRS Form 990, audited financial statements and Annual Reports, as applicable.

In contrast, there are some questionable Lyme nonprofits and charities with very ample and largely undisclosed funding sources. These Lyme nonprofits and charities share other characteristics. Most of them fail to encourage patients demand their rights to diagnosis and treatment options which meet international standards.

Their websites feature self-help tips including 'how to cope with being sick' and little to no leadership on how to prevent the medical marginalization. They do not encourage their members and patients take legal action against those who perpetrate human rights abuses and make few concrete suggestions to the change abusive patterns by medical personnel and establishments who obstruct diagnosis and treatment.

Most of these organizations have cozy relationships with the same government Actors responsible for harmful $Lyme Guidelines and policies. In many cases, they are selected by powerful $Lyme allies 'to represent the patients' while 'managing the expectations' of the patient population. In most cases, these organizations recommend patients accept Lyme Guidelines, Reports to legislators and other impactful documents which will maintain the harmful status quo.

They often employ tactics to reduce patient demands. As an example, UK Lyme patients were told by a Lyme advocacy organization to accept disability support instead of improved medical care because patients were never going to receive more than a short course of antibiotics.

Certain Lyme nonprofits in the US have said the lack of transparency surrounding the Working Group is 'not an issue' because patients are represented by them. Patients have been asked to support the 'progress made' by the Working Group even though the Working Group makes no recommendations to immediately open patient access to diagnostic and treatment options which already meet validated standards.

Some Lyme nonprofits are asking patients to support the House Bill 5878 *"To provide for a national strategy to address and overcome Lyme disease and other tickborne diseases, and for other purposes"* .

According to this Bill, the Working Group will play an influential role in future money flows. See *"(E) GRANTS.—The Secretary may award grants to, or enter into contracts or cooperative agreements with, public or private nonprofit entities to carry out activities under this paragraph."*

All the Working Group's subcommittees had clear scopes of work —to focus on reviewing the federal government's efforts in tickborne illnesses. Why did the Working Group's *Access to Care Services and Support to Patients Subcommittee* veer off their scope of work to identify and list Lyme nonprofits in their Report to the Working Group? Was this done to position these nonprofits to capture grants from the Bill? Most of the nonprofits listed have representatives in the Working Group and subcommittees. Did the Working Group decide to add this list of nonprofits to their draft Report to Congress to encourage and award $Lyme alliance?

Following the global announcement regarding ICD11 and the changes in the ICD Lyme codes, my analytics showed over one million hits. Information regarding the ICD11 Lyme codes has been shared across the globe by many hundreds of patient support groups, and many thousands of patient advocates and medical professionals.

Every week I receive hundreds of questions from patients in multiple nations asking how these codes can be used to access treatment, reimbursements for treatment and change Lyme Guidelines and policies.

I have not received one question from any member of these large, well-endowed 'patient advocacy groups' previously described. As of September 20, 2018, these patient advocacy organizations have posted nothing for their patient community regarding the Lyme ICD11 codes. In fact, their response to these historic and groundbreaking validations by WHO has been dead silence.

###

The $Lyme family well understands these new codes validate the same science they have been suppressing and may jeopardize profit streams and/or status for many Actors in the world of $Lyme. They are also aware this information is globally broadcast by WHO and the details are available to all persons who wish to review the WHO ICD11 digital platform.

They can do nothing to the erase the truth; a truth which shows evidence of their propaganda and corruption.

The ICD11 codes for Lyme are a slap in the face across the powers that be. They are more than a slap in the face; they threaten the entire $Lyme world.

As the HHS official in Liberia said, *'they are not going to be able to keep covering up the truth for much longer.'*

These code changes show there are too many people, in too many places, including critical decision-making roles, who know the realities of this disease and epidemic.

The World Health Organization does not build consensus for change until there is global buy in to favor change.

$Lyme has LOST its Global Grip.

Manipulation and Denial Around ICD

Expanding the ICD Lyme codes can result in tremendous benefit for patients and clinicians to improve access to diagnosis and treatment on a global scale.

There are, however, a series of challenges within the ICD at the national level. The US, Canada and Australia all modify the ICD codes. Many of these modifications are focused on making the language more precise in order to ensure reimbursements. In the case of Canada, the situation is more complex and appears to be firmly under the sinister control of $Lyme.

Unlike most countries where ICDs are managed in public domain, the Canadian ICD codes are owned by an independent nonprofit known as the Canadian Institute for Health Information (CIHI). A quick institutional analysis of CIHI shows this 'independent nonprofit' may be an 'Astroturf' front as CIHI's large executive board is almost entirely held by government officials from key health agencies.

This arrangement benefits the government of Canada. The government of Canada would be required by law to undergo a series of public stakeholder engagements and provide justifications to any modifications made to the ICD if they owned the codes.

An independent nonprofit, however, organized to do the government's bidding is under no such requirement. CIHI may therefore implement any and all government policy related to the ICD far from public scrutiny. Such policies could be reporting or not reporting cases of Lyme, and not reimbursing for Lyme treatment.

ICD10 version has been in place for approximately one decade and ICD10 recognizes three complications from Lyme. These include: M01.2 Arthritis due to Lyme; G01 Meningitis due to Lyme; and G63.0 Polyneuropathy due to Lyme.

However, under the control of the CIHI and its board of government officers, the Canadian version of ICD10 makes no reference whatsoever to these three complications and merely notes A69.2 Lyme Disease and disseminated Lyme, unspecified. This means that for well over a decade, it is probable the data on Canadians with Lyme meningitis, arthritis or polyneuropathies has not been collected. This indicates that many suffering from these complications have been ignored.

For one independent nonprofit, CIHI has unusually great power over the Canadian health system. According to its website, 'CIHI has the responsibility to maintain ICD-10-CA. All enhancements, addenda and errata are only official when approved by CIHI'.

US health insurers have a major role in obstructing reimbursements for treatment options following Lyme diagnosis. Despite there being ICD codes in place, it appears insurers make use of professional medical shills to act as expert witnesses to deny the diagnosis. The denial of the diagnosis results in subsequent treatment costs being offloaded onto the patient.

There are other arenas where the truth as represented by ICD11 must fight entrenched $Lyme interests. Such arenas include the halls of academia were medical training takes place and the increasing numbers of medical journals shown to be in the thrall of medical and scientific profiteering. $Lyme allies populate these spaces like mushrooms on rot due to decades of bias in grant awards and publications. Despite all the financial backing and preferential treatment, $Lyme propaganda is losing ground and the ICD11 is stark proof.

Fate loves the fearless.
—James Russell Lowell

Part Six
Global Mobilization

Realize that everything connects to everything else.
—Leonardo DaVinci

Chapter 14: Global Opportunities

$Lyme will not slink away and slither into a hidey hole because of ICD11. The World Health Organization has given powerful validation that Lyme is a serious and life threatening illness which damages the central nervous system and may cause multiple disabling late-stage complications.

The IDSA, CDC, DOD and most governments and medical societies across the globe were part of the ICD11 process. Therefore, representatives from the IDSA, CDC and $Lyme allies who dismiss the Lyme complications stated in the ICD11 codes will appear foolish, unprofessional and corrupt.

There are reasons this WHO code outcome is far more truthful than many Lyme policies. Unlike CDC, IDSA and Tickborne Diseases Working Group, WHO has strict requirements and practices for transparency and representation, making it almost impossible to erase inputs, suppress science and ignore advocates.

This powerful validation and ICD11 information can be used today by advocates to overturn policies and practices which deny diagnosis and treatment options to Lyme patients. ICD11 Lyme codes can be used to mount a globalized advocacy strategy against the wounded global $Lyme machine.

Know the Codes, Use the Codes

The ICD are adopted globally and can be used as a universal language for those who advocate against the medical marginalization and human rights abuses of persons with Lyme and Lyme-like illness.

This requires the codes be learned and disseminated among medical professionals, patients, care takers, policy makers, government and elected officials. Many officials recognize the relevance of WHO and therefore should be willing to engage on topics which have WHO support. The Lyme codes may assist advocates in building a strategic agenda for change. This book provides rationales and details regarding the ICD11 portrayal of a disease which is **not easy** to diagnose, treat and cure. The book's talking points and graphics are helpful tools for disseminating information on Lyme in ICD11.

Patients should take copies of the ICD11 Lyme codes to their medical practitioners and show WHO has recognized persistent Lyme can cause many serious complications. Patients with negative test results should ask for clinical diagnosis and access to treatment, as necessary.

The most effective advocacy approach uses human rights language to avoid the unending spiral of limiting medical debate. Emphasis on access to diagnosis and treatment for all, as opposed to expensive concierge services for the select few with big bucks, will help gain broader support .

Lastly, research 'for the future best' never takes precedence over addressing immediate need and suffering. Do not be fooled by research promises —immediate access to every diagnostic and treatment option which meets required state, national, regional or international standards is a human right.

You do not have to choose between research and care.

Demand Immediate Policy Change

The science supporting the changes in the ICD11 Lyme codes can be immediately deployed to demand policy revisions. The following two examples were selected because of their wide appeal to the general population.

Prevention of Dementia, Alzheimer's and other Neurodegenerative diseases

$Lyme allies and the misinformed say Alzheimer's, dementia and multiple neurodegenerative diseases such as MS, Parkinson's and ALS are skyrocketing and there are 'no cures'. ICD11 provides a strong path forward to counter this hopeless scenario. ICD11 officially recognizes '6D85.Y Dementia due to Lyme Disease' and '8A45.0Y Central Nervous System demyelination due to Lyme borreliosis'.

Now 'Prevention of Dementia, Alzheimer's and other Neurodegenerative diseases' requires new public health policies:

- No barriers to Lyme diagnosis are permitted for any person diagnosed with dementia, Alzheimer's, MS, ALS and/or Parkinson's disease.

- Unreliable Lyme serology tests means persons suffering from these complications should be given the option of empirical therapy for Lyme.

- No barriers to Lyme treatment options are permitted for any person diagnosed with Lyme-related MS, ALS, Parkinson's disease, dementia and/or Alzheimer's.

- Clinical diagnosis of Lyme and access to treatment options which meet internationally validated standards can stop or slow Lyme-related MS, ALS, Parkinson's disease, dementia and/or Alzheimer's.

Prevention of Lyme Beyond Tick Bites

'Prevention of Lyme' focuses on preventing tick bites. According to WHO's ICD11 codes, '1C1G.2 Congenital Lyme' recognizes Lyme can be transmitted from mother to child.

Now 'Prevention of Lyme' requires new public health policies:

- No barriers to Lyme diagnosis are permitted for pregnant women and women planning pregnancy.

- No barriers to Lyme treatment options are permitted for pregnant women and women planning pregnancy.

- Clinical diagnosis of Lyme and access to treatment options which meet internationally validated standards increase the chances for healthy babies, mothers and children.

Global Mobilization

The benefits from the new codes will only be realized when patients, advocates, medical and scientific professionals, and politicians are informed and undertake concerted political efforts to demand these potentially fatal complications be prevented, and their underlying infections be diagnosed and treated. The integration of this knowledge into health policies across the globe must begin today.

The global borreliosis epidemic demands a far reaching response from many sectors of society and government institutions beyond those responsible for public health. This comprehensive approach is required because $Lyme has breached and sullied many core institutions beyond the healthcare sector.

The following page contains the 2016 comprehensive list of actions recommended by the international all-voluntary Dream Team.

The recommendations on this list can be used by advocates at a local, state, regional, and global level to bring about change and enlist support from many groups outside the patient com-munity. These would include schools, sports clubs, farmers' associations, hunting clubs, landscapers, local businesses, local politicians, and so forth.

Declaration
Medical, Scientific, and Human Rights Leaders
Demand Changes to Address the Borreliosis Epidemic

Medical professionals, scientists, legal and human rights advocates from around the world demand key institutions responsible for public health and public welfare recognize and respond to the seriousness of the borreliosis epidemic. We now provide these institutions the following solutions and state our willingness to help them meet these goals.

Solutions
1. Increase public funding to improve Lyme and Lyme-like illness diagnostic tests. There should be a portion of this funding set aside for new innovators.
2. Until such tests are available, honor, support and accept the clinical diagnosis of Lyme and Lyme-like illness.
3. Create enabling environments for multiple innovative diagnostic tests to compete with those patents and reagents held by CDC and other institutions holding outdated patents.
4. Change the laws so government institutions and officials responsible for promoting scientific and medical innovations cannot be patent holders in the same arenas of competition.
5. Continue to modernize the WHO ICD codes for Lyme and Lyme-like illness to reflect the complexity and seriousness of the disease. Modernize the WHO's ICD codes for relapsing fever borreliosis.

6. Utilize the improved ICD codes to enhance the quality of and Lyme-like illness surveillance to:
   - inform public health policy
   - strengthen the 'One Health' synergy —to obtain optimal health of people, animals, and the environment
   - understand and prepare for the impact of climate change
7. Official recognition of complicated and persistent Lyme and Lyme-like illness is required.
8. Official recognition of physical disability caused by Lyme and Lyme-like illness is required.
9. Require national health systems and private insurers to recognize and provide treatment coverage for complicated and persistent forms of Lyme and Lyme-like illness. Qualifying treatments would include those which meet IOM criteria.
10. Stop the persecution of doctors who utilize clinical diagnosis and treatments which meet IOM criteria for Standards for Developing Trustworthy Clinical Practice Guidelines.
11. Penalize the slandering, libeling, stigmatizing and bullying of Lyme patients and those with Lyme-like illness.
12. Make the differential diagnosis of Lyme and Lyme-like illness part of standard medical assessments in countries where the diseases have been identified.
13. Integrate ICD11 Lyme codes and associated medical knowledge into medical training including pharmacists and nurses
14. The lack of differential diagnosis is particularly problematic for certain groups —such as the elderly. For example, untreated Lyme and Lyme-like illness symptoms can mimic conditions associated with aging, such as arthritis, dementia, vision and hearing loss.

15. Honor patients' rights to choose among treatment options and require medical professionals to inform patients of these choices.
16. Increase public funding for patient-centered research to improve diagnosis and treatments for and Lyme-like illness, other tickborne diseases and co-infections.
17. In many countries, children are among in the highest risk groups for Lyme and Lyme-like illness. Organize collective attention as to how the long-term health of these children can be preserved, their lives advanced, and their potential and dreams fulfilled.
18. Require public schools and universities to develop plans to accommodate students living with complicated and persistent forms of Lyme and Lyme-like illness.
19. Require public institutions to formulate how they will accommodate the needs of taxpayers living with Lyme and Lyme-like illness as well as their own employees living with this complex illness.
20. Engage private business and corporations in developing employer approaches to support employees who have debilitation or other limitations due to Lyme and Lyme-like illness.
21. Require all standing governmental committees for Lyme and Lyme-like illness research and policy have patient and caretaker stakeholder representation.

*If you want to tell people the truth,
make them laugh,
otherwise they'll kill you.*
— George Bernard Shaw

ENDNOTES

[1] I considered a Lyme diagnosis because a childhood friend and former medical professional with Johns Hopkins University suggested I be tested for Lyme; she also told me the standard treatment protocols promoted by the Infectious Diseases Society of America largely failed persons with late stage disseminated Lyme.

[2] I found a nurse practitioner who was willing to prescribe the therapies proposed by ILADS founding member Dr. Joe Burrascano; see <u>Advance Topics in Lyme disease Diagnostic Hints and Treatment Guidelines for Lyme and Other Tickborne Illnesses</u>, Sixteenth Edition, October, 2008, by Joseph J. Burrascano Jr, MD

[3] An MRI has shown I have brain lesions common to MS, however, following my long term antibiotic therapy for Lyme, my neurological 'MS symptoms' have, for the most part, disappeared.

[4] I have undertaken many international assignments for the US government to address corruption and ensure services are brought the most marginalized of persons.

[5] Cochrane was formed 25 years ago to summarize the best medical evidence from research to inform treatment choices. Cochrane has 11,000 members from more than 130 countries. Many within the international Cochrane community have expressed concern over the increasing influence of pharmaceutical and business interests within Cochrane. In an historic first for Cochrane, Gøtzsche was expelled in retaliation to a July 2018 article that criticized a publication by Cochrane Collaboration —Gøtzsche and two colleagues found their review of HPV vaccine documentation to be incomplete and biased.

[6] See IDSA website regarding policies and legislation that promote financial benefits to the members of IDSA.

[7] Joseph G. Jemsek, MD, FACP, AAHIVS. 2007 White Paper for Connecticut Attorney General Richard Blumenthal on Conflicts of Interest in the 2006 'Clinical Assessment, Treatment, and Prevention of Lyme Disease, Human Granulocytic Anaplasmosis, and Babesiosis: Clinical Practice Guidelines by the Infectious Diseases Society of America'.

[8] (page 56, BOX 3-1) Editors: Graham R, Mancher M, Wolman DM, Greenfield S, Steinberg E. Clinical Practice Guidelines We Can Trust. IOM (US) Committee on Standards for Developing Trustworthy Clinical Practice Guidelines; Washington (DC): National Academies Press (US); 2011. Web Source: http://www.nationalacademies.

[9] Patent No. 7605248 Recombinant constructs of *Borrelia* burgdorferi

[10] 2006 'Clinical Assessment, Treatment, and Prevention of Lyme Disease,

Human Granulocytic Anaplasmosis, and Babesiosis: Clinical Practice Guidelines by the Infectious Diseases Society of America'

[11] See public comments by Paul Auwaerter, the current IDSA President, on HHS website. https://www.hhs.gov/ash/advisory-committees/tickbornedisease/meetings/2018-07-24/written-public-comment/index.html —Reviewed 9.14.2018

[12] Cook M, Puri B. Commercial test kits for detection of Lyme borreliosis: A meta-analysis of test accuracy. International Journal of General Medicine. 2016; Volume 9:427–440. doi:10.2147/ijgm.s122313

[13] Schwarzwalder A, Schneider MF, Lydecker A, Aucott JN Sex differences in the clinical and serologic presentation of early Lyme disease: Results from a retrospective review. Gend Med. 2010 Aug;7(4):320-9. doi: 10.1016/j.genm.2010.08.002.

[14] The documentation of this collusion regarding the diagnostic tests is on record with the State of Connecticut and in US Congressional testimony.

[15] Sin Hang Lee graduated from Wuhan Medical College in China. After a residency-fellowship at Cornell-New York Hospital and Memorial Hospital for Cancer, Dr. Lee was certified by the American Board of Pathology and obtained the F.R.C.P.(C) degree in 1966. He was on the faculty of McGill University, then Yale University from 1968-2004 while practicing hospital-based pathology. He has over 70 publications from a career that has spanned nearly six decades.

[16] https://www.cdc.gov/ticks/miyamotoi.html —Reviewed 9.15.2018

[17] Numbers are based on CDC website estimates of infections and the percentage of person with debilitation and disability following treatment failure. —Reviewed 9.15.2018

[18] MUS has been repudiated by the American Psychiatric Association and deleted from the Diagnostic and Statistical Manual of Mental Disorders, Fifth Edition, is the principal guide for psychiatric disorders.

[19] Auwaerter PG, Bakken JS, Dattwyler RJ, Dumler JS, Halperin JJ, McSweegan E, Nadelman RB, O'Connell S, Shapiro ED, Sood SK, Steere AC, Weinstein A, Wormser GP. Antiscience and ethical concerns associated with advocacy of Lyme disease. Lancet Infect Dis. 2011 Sep;11(9):713-9. doi: 10.1016/S1473-3099(11)70034-2. PMID: 21867956

[20] On record with the Department of Health and Human Services' Office of Research Integrity, the Office of Civil Rights and multiple congressional and Senate offices.

[21] On CDC website (www.cdc.gov/lyme/treatment/index.html) it says go to this link "For details on research into "chronic Lyme disease" and long-term treatment trials sponsored by NIH, visit the National Institutes of Health Lyme Disease web site. On that NIH link (www.niaid.nih.gov/diseases-conditions/lyme-disease) it says: "To learn about risk factors for Lyme Disease and current prevention and treatment strategies visit the MedlinePlus Lyme Disease site (link is external) and Medline is under NIH/US National Library of Medicine. NIH/Medline links to UpToDate. Look under 'Treatments and

Therapies Lyme Disease Treatment' (Beyond the Basics) (UpToDate). On UpToDate, most of the language, e.g. "Treatment of Lyme disease", is lifted directly from the IDSA 2006 Guidelines, and of course references the 2006 IDSA Lyme Guidelines. The UpToDate authors also attack other treatment protocols that have met the IOM's internationally recognized standards for clinical practice Guidelines. —Reviewed 9.15.2018

[22] See research in public comments by Lorraine Johnson on HHS website. https://www.hhs.gov/ash/advisory-committees/tickbornedisease/meetings/2018-07-24/written-public-comment/index.html —Reviewed 9.15.2018

[23] https://eur-lex.europa.eu/legal-content/EN/TXT/PDF/?uri=CELEX:32018D0945&from=EN#page=29 —Reviewed 9.15.2018

[24] https://www.ncbi.nlm.nih.gov/pmc/articles/PMC5866998/ Johnson AL, Johnstone LK, 2 and Darko Stefanovski D, Cerebrospinal fluid Lyme multiplex assay results are not diagnostic in horses with neuroborreliosis. J Vet Intern Med. 2018 Mar-Apr; 32(2): 832–838. doi: 10.1111/jvim.15067 PMCID: PMC5866998 PMID: 29460492

[25] Henningsson AJ, Christiansson M, Tjernberg I, Löfgren S, Matussek, A Laboratory diagnosis of Lyme neuroborreliosis: a comparison of three CSF anti-*Borrelia* antibody assays Eur J Clin Microbiol Infect DisDOI 10.1007/s10096-013-2014-6

[26] Short description of Morten Lanne's method of detection https://www.youtube.com/watch?v=QTlcgCql2k0

[27]   Morten M. Laane, Ivar Mysterud. A simple method for the detection of live *Borrelia* spirochaetes in human blood using classical microscopy techniques. Biological and Biomedical Reports, 2013, 3(1), 15-28 http://counsellingme.com/microscopy/Mysterud AndLaane.pdf

[28] Dr. Bakken is a consultant in infectious diseases at St. Luke's Hospital and a clinical associate professor at the University of Minnesota Medical School Duluth. Dr. Bakken served as chair of the IDSA's State and Regional Societies Board and became the President of the IDSA in 2016. Bakken has served on the IDSA Diagnostics Task Force and was a contributor to the 2006 IDSA Guidelines for Lyme borreliosis.

[29] Dr. David Martz, an American internal medicine specialist, hematologist and oncologist published how his Lyme was misdiagnosed as motor neuron disease and responded to extended antimicrobial therapies for lyme infection. David's case is published. Harvey, WT, Martz, D. Motor neuron disease recovery associated with IV ceftriaxone and anti-Babesia therapy. Acta Neurologica Scandinavica. Volume 115 Issue – 2. 2007. Blackwell Publishing Ltd. UR - http://dx.doi.org/10.1111/j.1600-0404.2006.00727.x

[30] Further human rights detias can be found in the The Situation of Human Rights Defenders of Lyme and Relapsing Fever Borreliosis Patients: Edition One, March 6, 2018. Authors: Jenna Luché-Thayer, Holly Ahern, Robert Bransfield,

Joseph Burrascano, Anne Fierlafijn, Theresa Denham, Huib Kraaijeveld, Jennifer Kravis, Mualla McManus, Clement Meseko, Jack Lambert, Sin Hang Lee, Kenneth Liegner, Christian Perronne, Kenneth Sandström, Ursula Talib, Torben Thomsen, Jim Wilson. Expert Reviewers: Gabriela Barrios, Barbaros Cetin, Joseph Jemsek, Jose Lapenta, Natasha Rudenko, Armin Schwarzbach. Advisors: Cees Hamelink, Astrid Stuckelberger. To contact the principal author, email jennaluche@gmail.com ISBN-10: 1722988061 ISBN-13: 978-1722988067 CreateSpace Independent Publishing Platform July 14, 2018

[31] June 5, 2018 PRESS RELEASE: Corruption and Human Rights Violations Against Lyme Doctors, Scientists and Parents Now on United Nations Record https://www.linkedin.com/pulse/corruption-human-rights-violations-against-lyme-now-luche-thayer/

31547036R00072

Printed in Poland
by Amazon Fulfillment
Poland Sp. z o.o., Wrocław